Experience and Participation

Report of the Review Group on the Youth Service in England

Presented to Parliament
by the Secretary of State for Education and Science
by Command of Her Majesty
October 1982

THOMPSON Report

LONDON
HER MAJESTY'S STATIONERY OFFICE
£7.75 net

Cmnd. 8686

To: The Secretary of State for Education and Science
From: Alan Thompson

"Experience and Participation"
The Report of the Review Group on the Youth Service

I have pleasure in submitting to you the report of the Review Group set up by your predecessor in January 1981. It has been agreed unanimously by the Group; and we believe this very unanimity reflects a widespread feeling, which we have sensed both in the youth service and in many sections of the general public, that the time is ripe for a re-statement of the objectives of youth provision and a renewed commitment to it.

We trust that the publication of this report will give focus to this feeling, and lead to specific action along the lines recommended.

August 1982

To: A Thompson Esq CB
From: Sir Keith Joseph

Thank you for your letter of 26 August enclosing the report of the Review Group on the Youth Service, "Experience and Participation".

Your report is a timely and far-reaching study of the ways in which the youth service is helping young people already, and offers some important recommendations for its development to cope better with their current and likely future needs. My colleagues and I will be giving careful consideration to your proposals.

In the meantime, I should like to express my gratitude to you and to all the members of your Group for completing a thorough and comprehensive study so promptly.

14 September 1982

TABLE OF CONTENTS

INTRODUCTION

i. We were set up by the Secretary of State for Education and Science in January 1981 to conduct a review of the Youth Service in England with the following terms of reference:

(1) To report on present provision, both statutory and voluntary;

(2) To consider whether available resources could be deployed more effectively; and, in the light of this,

(3) To assess the need for legislation.

The circumstances which we understand to have been the immediate cause of our being appointed were as follows. In the 1979–80 session of Parliament a Private Member's Bill put forward by Mr. Trevor Skeet MP attracted a great deal of interest and support both within the House of Commons and outside it. Its purpose was to place the Youth Service on what the sponsors felt to be a more secure and comprehensive basis. Though it failed in the end in the form presented to win the support of the Government, the Ministerial spokesman in a subsequent adjournment debate on the subject in July 1980 promised that a review would be set up to study youth provision, including the need for statutory change. Hence in particular the third of our terms of reference.

ii. It may well be thought, however, that a review such as this was in any case over-due. There have been many changes in society and in government services since the Youth Service was reviewed in 1958–60 by the Albermarle Committee, and it was time to take a look not only at the Youth Service as such but also at the context in which it operates. We formed the view early in our enquiry that, while the "Youth Service" must be taken to mean the system of clubs, recreational facilties, centres and other services provided for young people by local authorities and voluntary organisations, we could not assess this provision properly if we restricted our attention to it alone. There are two main reasons for this. In recent years there has been a movement towards a broader concept of youth provision based on a recognition of the fact that the personal development of young people is influenced and conditioned by a whole range of factors in society. Hence a number of local education authorities have changed the title of their Youth Services to one such as "Youth and Community Service". This change is in most cases not just a nominal one: it betokens a broadening of the functions of the Service, which brings it into contact with other related services. The second reason follows from this. It has become clear to us that the Youth Service cannot be looked at in isolation. Apart from in schools and further education colleges, work with groups of young people and with individuals is undertaken by the social services departments of many authorities, services which provide for recreation and leisure, the probation services and the police, while over the past half-a-dozen years a massive incursion into the field has been made by the Manpower Services Commission. These developments have created uncertainty, not so much about the central core of the Youth Service's work as about its extent, scope, future, and especially its relationship with other bodies.

iii. It seemed to us that a proper assessment of present Youth Service provision would have to involve a thorough examination of what was being done both within these boundaries and beyond them; and we have found that this called for a fundamental study of objectives and methods as well as performance. To this end we sought information and views from a wide range of organisations: those from whom we have received submissions are listed in Appendix B. We also visited a variety of provision in both the statutory and voluntary sectors and spoke to a number with experience in the Service. This process aroused widespread interest in the field, and we though it right to issue, with the agreement of the Secretary of State, an interim statement in order to make clear our approach (Appendix C). It was at this stage that one of our number, Ms. Jan McKenley, joined us. It was felt that her youth and experience both as a member of the black community and in working with young people in an inner city would bring fresh points of view to our discussions. We also considered it desirable to seek the views of young people themselves as represented to us in the written submissions, to which we naturally attached great weight, and also, more directly, through meetings and conversations with young people and by commissioning an opinion survey of young people's attitudes by a commercial market research firm, Q-Search Ltd. The scope of this survey is outlined in Appendix D, and the results are referred to frequently throughout our report. We believe that they may be found to be of wider interest outside the immediate context of our enquiry, and we have therefore recommended that the DES should seek to arrange publication of the findings.

iv. Our report falls into three parts. In the first part, we examine those features of present-day society which most affect young people, and describe the needs which young people have and the ways in which these are being met by various agencies, including the Youth Service. In the second part, we consider the aims and methods of the Youth Service, first as these are seen by others including the many bodies and individuals who gave evidence to us, and then as we ourselves view them. This part concludes with a picture as we see it of the essential features which the Youth Service should display if it is to be an effective force in the future. In the third part, we look at some important resource considerations, including the staffing and administration of the Service, and at the question of legislation.

v. We cannot conclude this brief introduction without recording our thanks to the Department's assessors, first Mr. M. B. Baker and then Mr. Peter Emms who succeeded him, and particularly our assessor from H. M. Inspectorate, Mr. Edwin Sims, who freely gave us the benefit of his own stored wisdom and experience and also afforded us access to the experience of colleagues in the Inspectorate. We also wish to thank our secretary, Mr. Mark Todd HMI. He was assisted first by Mr. Neil Flint and later by Miss Katherine Fleay, both from the staff of the DES, and our thanks go also to them and the clerical staff who helped them. Without their dedicated work, well beyond the call of duty, this report could not have been written. Finally, we wish to express our gratitude to all the many bodies who helped us by replying to our questionnaire and enquiries. The written submissions which we received were detailed and illuminating; and if our report has merit this is due in large measure to the quality of the input from the field. We thank the government departments who provided detailed information and sent representatives to our meetings. We thank also those members and officers of local authorities and voluntary bodies who received us on our visits, made sure that we were comfortable, and took endless pains to show us what we wanted to see.

PART 1   WHAT THE YOUTH SERVICE DOES

CHAPTER 1:   SOCIETY AND YOUTH—A GENERATION OF CHANGE

"He that will not apply new remedies must expect new evils; for time is the greatest innovator." (Bacon)

Current period of rapid change. Brief sketch of historical developments from which the present Youth Service has emerged to face this change.

1.1   All ages see themselves as ages of change, sometimes change and decay, sometimes change and growth. We are living through a period of rapid transformation in many of the ideas and characteristics which make our society what it is. There is much in this process which is liberating and invigorating; but there is also waste, loss, frustration. Young people feel both aspects keenly, because it is in the nature of youth to aspire to the status of adulthood; and, if the very landmarks of adult life, its freedoms and its responsibilities, are shifting, the experience of youth is the more difficult and problematic even where it seems most full of hope.

1.2   Society has always had aspirations for its young people, though it has rarely acknowledged the aspirations of the young themselves. Young people are in a state of transition from dependency to independence; and adult people, acting in the name of various agencies in society, intervene constantly in their lives and in this process. At most times in the past it has not been thought that the young need have any say in this process. Today we are beginning to see the process as a collusive one, and this is one of the important changes in outlook which has taken place over the period during which the Youth Service has achieved recognition as a valid and distinct set of institutions and ideas.

1.3   The term "Youth Service" itself is not very old—no older, it would seem, than the Board of Education's celebrated Circular 1486, issued at the beginning of the 1939—45 war. The process of intervention is of course far older than that, and has inevitably reflected the changing moods and outlooks of adult society. Institutions have been created in response to needs perceived from various social, political and religious viewpoints; and, while aims and methods have altered along with changes in society, a natural loyalty and conservatism has tended to keep old forms and structures alive, so that the Youth Service of today carries traces of several stages of past thinking and practice. The problem for today's policymakers is to decide which aspects of this varied tradition are relevant to the needs of young people in today's society. It seems appropriate therefore to begin our study with a brief historical sketch of the main phases of development of the Youth Service, as a preliminary to considering what needs it has to meet today.

The Victorian Founders: Moral Improvement

1.4   The oldest tradition in youth provision, and one which is still perhaps a major constituent in the general public conception of the Service, has its roots in the concern for moral improvement in the late Victorian period. This inspired energetic and public-spirited people of good social standing to set up organi-

3

sations—local, national and world-wide—with the object of enabling young people to identify with socially acceptable patterns of activity. One type of organisation in particular had its origin in this social environment: large-scale movements on a national and international basis which developed to provide a means of association, a corporate basis for physical activity, a regular pattern of life, and in some cases a specific religious element.

1.5 This type of approach endured as the mainstream of youth provision for a long time. Though the years just after the First World War saw a start in public intervention with the institution by the Board of Education of Juvenile Organisations Committees, it was still the dominant characteristic of youth provision in the 1920s and 1930s—a period of great stress and despondency for large sections of the population of this country. The Youth Service (though rarely thought of as such) was seen as offering some defence against poverty, depression and disease, and as helping to bring some cohesion into a society whose values were widely thought to be under threat. Physical fitness, healthy pursuits (preferably in the open air), and the cultivation of social virtues—all organised by dedicated volunteers—were the hall-marks of the oldest stratum in the system we have come to call the Youth Service.

World War II: The Growth of Organised Welfare

1.6 Circular 1486, issued by the Board of Education in November 1939 under the title 'The Service of Youth', still powerfully evokes memories of a painful yet oddly exhilarating period of social awakening. "Today the black-out, the strain of war and the disorganisation of family life", says the Circular, "have created conditions which constitute a serious menance to youth". The Board of Education was given responsibility for youth welfare; a National Youth Committee was set up; financial assistance was provided, through voluntary organisations, to help clubs and centres re-open in hired or borrowed premises, to provide equipment and to secure "competent leaders and instructors". Youth activities were still seen as mainly the province of voluntary bodies, but local education authorities were urged to help in vaious ways, e.g. by making school premises available. The Circular recognised a need for local education authorities and voluntary bodies to co-operate through "local Youth Committees", the local authority being responsible for servicing the committee and providing accommodation for it. The first duty of the proposed committees was to "ascertain the local needs" and "to formulate an ordered policy"; and, while much of the phraseology of the Circular has an antique ring, it is not without interest that it acknowledged that, "in order to ensure that free and direct expression might be given to the views of youth", it might be desirable for some respresentation on the committees to be given "… to young people of both sexes, not necessarily connected with any particular youth organisation". Finally, the Circular saw the Service of Youth, "too long a neglected part of the educational field", as having an equal status with the other educational services conducted by the local education authorities.

Post-War Reconstruction: Uncertainty of Aim as the Pace Quickens

1.7 The stimulus of Circular 1486 was successful, and Circular 13 of November 1944, issued at the start of that intense period of educational reconstruction

4

which followed the Education Act 1944, paid tribute to "the energy and efforts of Local Eduation Authorities and their Youth Committees, and of the voluntary organisations" for having "combined to bring about a substantial expansion of provision, despite all the handicaps imposed by war conditions". After the difficulties of the immediate post-war years, a mood of optimism pervaded the country in the early 1950s, soon to be tempered by a realisation that far-reaching changes in society were afoot. The Youth Service of the period had its aims defined in a well-known formulation made by Lord Redcliff-Maud, then Permanent Secretary of the Ministry of Education, at a Ditchley conference in 1951:

> "to offer individual young people in their leisure time opportunities of various kinds, complementary to those of home, formal education and work, to discover and develop their personal resources of body, mind and spirit and thus the better equip themselves to live the life of mature, creative and responsibile members of a free society".

This definition which comprehensively recapitulated pre-war and wartime experience has insights which are of enduring value today, but it ignored too much. Towards the end of that decade, compulsory national service came to an end; two channels of television began to compete for the attention of the population, expanding visual and emotional horizons; full employment and rising wages were creating a "teenage market" which the commercial world set out to serve; and there were signs of an emerging teenage culture, so-called, which did not appear necessarily to accept all the values of adult authority. Uncertainty grew over the proper role of the Youth Service, in particular over whether it should be working mainly with those who came to it of their own volition, or with those who had hitherto been and still were outside its scope. As we shall see, this debate has continued ever since. At the end of the 1950s, the Government's response was to set up the Albemarle Committee, which reported in 1960.

Albemarle: The Classic post-1944 Approach

1.8   The Albermarle Committee completed its work remarkably quickly and its principal recommendations were speedily and enthusiastically accepted. This was perhaps because it was working in a period of buoyant educational expenditure and took the "classical" post-Education Act 1944 view about what should be done to put an educational sector on the map. Strong emphasis was placed on the development of clubs and centres, a sizeable building programme was launched to ensure suitable premises for an expanded number of them, measures were taken to promote the training and supply of full-time professional youth leaders, and the Youth Service Development Council (YSDC) was set up to oversee progress and to consolidate the partnership between LEAs and voluntary bodies. The Committee was conscious of those people who were not attracted to club activity. These were described as "the unattached", and an experimental programme was recommended in order to reach them and, if possible, turn their steps towards some form of "association" (one of the key words of the report). In physical terms, including staffing, the Albemarle Report did an immense service to the youth movement: conceptually it left behind it a host of loose ends which were to emerge rapidly as major problems in the following decade.

5

The 1960s: High Tide of Educational Expansion, Youth Culture and Immigration

1.9   The 1960s were probably one of the most optimistic periods that this country has ever known. Energy was cheap, unemployment was low, all the educational indicators were moving upwards, prosperity seemed assured, with only momentary intervals of "stop/go". A major expansion took place in the higher and further education sectors. Yet at the same time the prevailing mood of "you-never-had-it-so-good" opportunism threw into sharp relief the problems of disadvantaged youth. Outbreaks of violence became far from rare, always greeted with pained surprise by adult authority. The various forms of adolescent deviance shown by a minority attracted unfailing attention from the media, which presented a negative image of all young people.

1.10   A new factor appeared on the scence—the possibly divisive consequences of immigration and multi-ethnic communities. The British public, themselves the product of as complete a racial mixture as it is possible to imagine, seemed unaware till now that the process was still continuing. The Hunt Report, published in 1967 on 'Immigrants and the Youth Service', recommended a multi-racial, integrationist approach for the Youth Service, and viewed separate provision as generally undesirable—a strategy which, as we shall see, stood no realistic chance of success and seems with hindsight to have been based on false premises.

1.11   Some initiatives by the YSDC and studies by other bodies served to highlight the problems which Albermarle had pointed to but not taken fully into account, such as the behaviour patterns associated with deprivation, under-achievement and rejection. Along with the realisation of this conceptual failure there was a substantial beginning of experimental work in so-called "detached" modes, in an attempt to minister to the "unattached".

'Youth and Community Work in the 1970s: Lack of Direction in a Colder Climate

1.12   The 1970s started with a report prepared by the YSDC which recognised many of the strains and stresses which had emerged into prominence since Albermarle, but failed to carry conviction with the Government or to evoke a consistent response from the Youth Service. The one thing which the report did perhaps achieve was to give such an impetus to the linking of youth work with community development that many LEAs reorganised their services and changed their names. But, though the report dealt comprehensively with the many new developments which were taking place in such matters as community service and other forms of involvement in community affairs, it is to be feared that a policy vacuum increasingly made itself felt as the decade went on. There were a number of reasons for this. The local government reorganisation of 1974 made local policy-makers uncertain of their roles; increasing financial stringency inhibited national leadership and compelled departments to concentrate more on shoring up selectively what had been achieved than on breaking new ground; in the face of increasing problems in the inner cities, of social and economic disadvantage and racial discrimination, the Youth Service seemed to have no generally acknowledged role. Various initiatives were taken by the DES

6

in the mid-1970s: a discussion document was issued in 1975 to stimulate debate on the future of the Service and particularly its role with the disadvantaged, and subsequently in 1977 the Youth Service Forum was set up to provide a focus for discussion of various issues. But this failed to give a sustained lead, and there was no consensus as to what the Youth Service should be doing or how it should be doing it. Indeed it began to seem as though there was not one Youth Service but many. The growth of professionalised social services departments meant that social workers were seen to be organising group activities for young people "at risk", which were not easily distinguished from Youth Service work. Towards the end of the decade a new problem of daunting proportions appeared – long-term and structural unemployment, bearing down with particular severity upon young people. As youth unemployment increased, the Manpower Services Commission developed programmes backed by large inputs of public money which often successfully involved the very "unattached" youth who formed the clientele of the newer manifestations of Youth Service work. It is significant that the decade witnessed no less than four separate attempts, through Private Members' Bills, to tackle the statutory basis of the Youth Service and make it more comprehensive and mandatory.

1.13   We thus come, at the conclusion of this brief survey, to the circumstances in which the Review Group was set up, and it is now appropriate to consider in more detail what specific features of society and what emerging needs of young people we shall have to take into account in reaching conclusions about what the Youth Service is doing and should be doing. This will be the theme of the next chapter.

CHAPTER 2:   YOUTH AND SOCIETY—THE SITUATION TODAY

Positive and negative features in society as they affect young people. What young people themselves think of these. The gap between expectations and reality.

2.1   Most of the bodies and individuals who have given evidence to us have commented on the main features as they see them of the society in which young people have to make their way. In doing so they have tended to stress the negative features, pointing out the various ways in which our society is becoming a more difficult and dangerous place for the young to grow up in than was the case for former generations. This view is understandable and, so far as it goes, no doubt accurate. But it is necessary to remember the positive side of the balance sheet. Young people today are in general healthier than they were in the past, they are better educated, they have wider horizons and more opportunities. They are better protected against the worst things that can befall families—starvation, disease, cruelty, harsh working conditions, untimely death. These improvements, inestimable though they are, do not however necessarily go with steadier and more complete personal development. It is the latter factor which is the concern of the Youth Service; and, in order to see what is happening in that respect, we have to try to take a balanced view of what society does to and for young people, and of what the young people make of it.

2.2   Against the positive features of modern society noted above must be set a number of factors which are, to say the least, perplexing and confusing to adults, and which must seem all the more menacing to those who are still reaching out for a secure identity. We do not propose to go into these in detail, because it is not our job to write a sociological analysis. A mention of a few of the topics most frequently discussed in the media, in public debate and in the evidence we have received will suffice to show how ambivalent popular conceptions and attitudes are.

2.3   It is generally accepted, for example, that society is more *mobile* than it was, both physically and in matters of life-style. Sons and daughters less frequently follow their parents' occupations or live within the same community as their parents. Coupled with this is the frequent complaint that the *family* is declining as an institution. No doubt this is true in the sense that in general families are smaller and meet together (*i.e.* as an extended family) less often. Divorce and remarriage are more common; as a result, more children live with single parents or have a number of step-parents. But it is by no means clear to what extent these changes in the family, or in social mobility, really do limit or injure the experience of the adolescent. There has also been a decline in the sense of belonging to a *community*. There are specific reasons for this: the break-up of established communities in the interests of improving the physical environment, changes in the pattern and location of employment, and so on. The old certainly often speak with longing of the 'neighbourliness' of the places where they used to live. But again there are gains as well as losses here. There are areas where there has been positive rejuvenation. It is indeed true that for some the *physical environment* has not only changed but worsened; and no account of the situation of modern youth would be complete which did not recognise that for many of them

their immediate environment is devoid of physical a[...]
scope for pleasurable activity or adventure, and is som[...]
and incitements to violence. Unfortunately this was o[...]
people in the past. What is indisputable about this situ[...]
people are deeply affected by factors such as these a[...]
obstacle to their own personal development.

2.4   There are other features of our society which also ten[...]
the development of a secure sense of identity in young peopl[...] ...*materi-*
alistic society, given to measuring success by the number of t[...] which people
acquire. A whole industry is devoted to persuading people that they must have
this or that product, and to creating *anxiety* in the minds of those who do not
have it. Another industry, the media, often feeds on the anxiety with which it
manages to surround the events of our daily lives.

The Concerns of Young People

2.5   So far we have mentioned only general factors. There are, however, a
number of specific issues which impinge on the lives of young people; and in
order to learn what these are we have only to listen to what young people say
about the things that worry them. From what we have heard in our conversations
with young people, from the evidence presented to us by their organisations, and
from our opionion survey, it is possible to construct a remarkably consistent
picture.

2.6   *Unemployment*. This is not the place to argue alternative models of future
economic growth: it is sufficient to say that practically all commentators seem to
be agreed that the present trends in unemployment will continue for some time.
We shall be referring later to the steps which are being taken to mitigate the effect
on young people, and to what the Youth Service is doing and should do. Half of
those leaving school at the minimum age have, at the present time, little prospect
of getting a job, though they have a guaranteed place on a scheme funded by the
Manpower Services Commission. The point we make here is that the largest
growing group of long-term unemployed is in the 18–25 age-group, and relatively little is being done for them. The possibility of being unemployed, or the
actual experience of unemployment, is without doubt the chief worry of the
great majority of young people today. Throughout his or her conscious life,
work will have been held up as the essential badge of adulthood. It stands for the
end of dependence and the beginnings of real responsibility and freedom. It
brings with it financial means, status and the chance to choose within a range of
opportunities. It also combines in itself many of the kinds of experience which
are requisite for personal development. Its absence is the more keenly felt; and it
is meaningless to say to the youngster who has no employment that the "work
ethic" is over-valued in our society. Faced with the challenge of continuing high
rates of unemployment, it may be that society will evolve new patterns of work
and leisure and new approaches to employment. But in the meantime many
young people are being denied the opportunity of financial independence and
with it many of the most important attributes of adulthood.

2.7   *Racism*. By racism we mean the manifestation of a negative attitude
towards an ethnic group in the community, accompanied by discriminatory

9

...art of individuals or institutions. Racism has become more signi-
...s country since parts of it have become much more racially mixed
...s the case up to, say, the late 1950s. Before then there were of course
...ly groups in particular areas who had entered this country from other lands,
bringing their own distinctive traditions, language and appearance; and there
were first and second generation young people from all these communities. But
they were relatively few within the total numbers in their age-groups. The large-
scale immigration of family groups especially of Asian and Afro-Caribbean
origin since the early 1960s has meant that these groups form a significant and
sometimes a dominant proportion of the population in some areas, especially in
large industrial conurbations. These peoples along with groups already indige-
nous looked for, and were officially assured they had, equal rights and an equal
place in society with those of traditional British origin. Though there were
obviously distinctive cultural traits which they wished to preserve, they looked
forward to being part of the community. They looked on Britain as a homeland,
and their young people are already predominantly of British birth. Unfortunately it does not appear that British society was as prepared to assimilate these
peoples as they were to be assimilated. Deep-seated attitudes are no doubt in
some cases compounded by feelings of insecurity and resentment springing from
lack of good housing, educational disadvantage and a shortage of jobs. The
undeniable fact is that there is a significant amount of racial prejudice and racial
discrimination, and it is the effect of this on young people which we have to keep
in mind. For the young people within an ethnic community the experience of
racism may result in frustration, anger and despair leading possibly to a deep-
seated alienation. They have indeed to face many serious problems associated,
for example, with job opportunities, relations with the police, and the active
antagonism of extremist right-wing groups. It is important to recognise that this
effect spreads far wider than the immediate consequences for young members of
ethnic communities. Racism damages those who practise it as well as those who
suffer from it. It is a deep tragedy for British society that the cultural diversity
which should be a source of enjoyment and enrichment is liable to give rise to
expressions of violence, harassment and antipathy which impoverish and
threaten the lives of many and especially young people.

2.8 *Homelessness*. Though our survey shows that young people in general
value their homes and spend a lot of their time there, quite a number leave home
for long or short periods for a variety of reasons—not only because of family
conflicts, personal crises, tensions arising from overcrowding and other
emergencies, but also for reasons which are part of the process of growing up,
such as a desire to be independent. We have been faced with evidence of this in
rural areas just as much as in the inner cities. Serious problems arise, even where
the young people concerned are in employment, because of the shortage of
suitable accommodation and its high cost. Young people are not in general seen
as a priority group for housing. Young people give homelessness a high place
amongst the factors which affect their personal development.

2.9 These three problems—unemployment, racism and homelessness—figure
predominantly in all the representations we have received from young people,
but other factors, no less significant than these in their impact on particular individuals, may be mentioned. Many young people worry about their *education*,

about their level of achievement and their relationships at school and college; for many, schooling will not have been the enlarging experience that we often like to think it is. Many feel that there is little logic at present in the pattern of *age-thresholds* governing many aspects of work, education, leisure and domestic rights. Some young people feel that the *police* discriminate against them. *Leisure provision* for young people is often inaccessible and expensive. In rural areas especially, but also on large isolated housing estates, the lack of public *transport* and its high cost is a prime cause of isolation, depriving young people of activity and companionship. For many young people, boys as well as girls, attitudes in society towards the appropriate roles of *men and women* are seen as changing and confused. Some girls in particular feel that their personal development is considered relatively unimportant. For both sexes, sexual relations are a source of anxiety as well as bewilderment. Finally, mention must be made again of the growth of *extremist political organisations*, some of which set out deliberately to capture the allegiance of young people. The impact of these organisations is as damaging to those young people whom they succeed in winning over as to those who are the victims of their attentions.

2.10   The pressures on young people are in some cases the same as the pressures on adults. But young people are more vulnerable and need help in acquiring the outlook and coping skills which older people have. The situation is critical for society generally because the young of today are the citizens of tomorrow, who will have been strongly influenced by their adolescent experience.

2.11   The key to much that we are about to say lies in the gulf, vividly apparent to many young people, between the ideals and the realities of society. Schooling, for example, is presented as a preparation for life and subsequent employment. For many it brings real opportunities, but for some, disappointment and the stigma of failure. Moreover, some of the variations in school experience appear to mirror divisions in society itself, so that schooling comes to seem for some not the ladder of opportunity it was held up to be, but a foretaste of the frustrations which will be experienced later on. The experience of unemployment may be a test and a challenge, but it may equally produce a strong awareness of the futility of growing up into society's "ideal person"—well-educated and hardworking, when neither good education nor employment are real possibilities.

2.12   Outside school and work, young people have to bear the image of being beyond the control and immune to the influence of parents and other responsible adults. This picture is wildly exaggerated by the media. Our opinion survey has shown how strong an influence parents and relatives continue to have; and a certain tension between parents and children is normal and reasonable. There is a good deal of hypocrisy about, and young people often feel that they are the victims of "double standards" and are not valued as individuals.

2.13   Our survey has also shown that young people are well aware that progression to maturity is marked by a growth in both freedom and responsibility. Only a caring personal relationship can guarantee both. Problems arise in many areas of behaviour—in sexual relations, in the resort to alcohol and drugs, in relations with the law—when this progression is monitored not through personal relationships with caring adults, but through the more impersonal manifestations of

11

social observance and "law and order". The gap between expectation and reality then widens, irrationalities and inequalities become harder to bear, the young person may begin to feel an "outsider" in society, and a process of alienation is set on foot. This may lead in extreme cases to a rage against society, which may find expression in delinquency or violence, or more often in apathy and disillusion which may ultimately be equally destructive of the young person concerned and of the society of which he or she is part.

Lessons for the Youth Service

2.14   In this chapter we have tried to hold the balance between the negative and positive aspects of modern society. In doing so we have paid particular attention to what young people themselves have said to us. We certainly do not accept that the outlook is bad for all of them. Many young people continue to enter into adult society without undue difficulty or strain, as they have always done.

2.15   Nevertheless the negative factors are significant and cannot be brushed aside. For those young people who are affected by them it is important that the Youth Service should address the question of how to help them to react positively and constructively. This may be done partly by relieving the incidence of the factors involved and partly by developing in the young people concerned the capacity to play an active part in altering their condition. For those young people this is going to be a crucial part of their personal development. But the fact that a significant proportion of their peers suffer multiple disadvantages is also an important fact for *all* young people, and one which should inform the *general* experience of transition from dependency to adulthood. In considering its contribution to the personal development of young people in general, the Youth Service must bear particularly in mind the negative experiences of some of them, because young people must be helped to achieve a comprehensive and realistic sense of identity with society and an understanding of all its aspects.

CHAPTER 3: PERSONAL DEVELOPMENT AND HOW IT IS ACHIEVED

An analysis of personal development and of the crucial importance of experience. Role of the Youth Service in enlarging and extending experience. Other sources of experience: family, neighbourhood, school, work and commercial provision.

3.1 Statements about the Youth Service which attempt to specify the needs of young people and how these are to be met have often resorted to descriptions of the qualities and attributes which the proposers think young people aspire to, or should aspire to, which they think society wants them to have, and which they think their particular methods will inculcate—qualities such as self-confidence, temperance, discipline, understanding of others and so on.

3.2 Descriptions of this kind are valid, but they are neither analytical nor practical. They afford no clue as to how the activities in question actually help young people. In what follows we try to make clear the processes by which youth work and work by other agencies assist the personal development of young people. Taken together, these processes constitute a young person's social education.

3.3 As we have seen in chapter 2, young people are not slow to respond when asked to say what their chief concerns are. Their views on what it means to be an adult are interesting and important. To them it means responsibilities as well as freedoms, relationships as well as possessions. Both introspection and analysis suggest that what underlies this language is a desire for a change in relationships. Young people say that above all they want to ''grow up''—they aspire to the stage next ahead of them. The stages of human development are defined in terms of progress in relationships of which the more important are the following:

relationships with self,

relationships with parents and other significant adults,

relationships with friendship groups,

relationships with a particular partner,

relationships with colleagues in a school or work setting,

relationships to a wider society, and

relationships with an ultimate of some kind.

This list is of course equally characteristic of the adult state, but what matters for young people is the *change* in these relationships as they move from a state of dependency to a state of independence or interdependence.

3.4 This is highly abstract language. Relationships are not experienced in a pure form. They come in packages all mixed up together; or, to use another metaphor, they are the threads of which a particular piece of experience is made up. It is the experience itself which is actually felt and encountered, and it contains within itself many types of relationships. So if we ask what causes relationships to change and develop, we can only say 'experience'. This is also the commonly received wisdom—it is experiences which fashion men and women, not teaching and not native wit. People achieve change by living through particular kinds of situation. This is not to say that teaching has no place at all in the development of relationships, but there must be careful judgement about when to employ it.

3.5   The word "experience" is used here in a broad sense. The kinds of experience which contain within themselves the potentiality of changing relationships are basic and yet fully recognisable, e.g.:

   the experience of being valued and accepted as a person,

   the experience of measuring oneself against others,

   the experience of making choices and seeing them through,

   the experience of enduring and living with hard reality,

   the experience of playing a part in a common enterprise,

   the experience of being responsible to and for others,

   the experience of receiving, giving and sharing ideas, and

   the experience of perceiving others' needs.

It is obvious that experiences such as these arise from many different sources, from home and family life, from social intercourse in peer groups, from education, from work. It is obvious too that they will vary greatly in quality, kind and degree. It may well be that, in some situations, family life, ordinary social intercourse and the process of earning a living may provide the ideal "mix" of experience for particular individuals. But in general it has not been so. The traditional role of the Youth Service has been to supplement the modes of experience which young people encounter in their ordinary lives. This is clear when one reads the declared aims of such organisations as the Scouts and Guides, the National Association of Boys' Clubs and others. This is not of course to say that we explicitly endorse the methods used by any particular organisation.

3.6   If this analysis is correct and if the Youth Service has the function of enlarging and extending the experience of young people in certain critical ways, a number of conclusions follows.

3.7   The first and most obvious is that the Youth Service does not stand alone. There are other agencies at work, all aiming to affect the experiential environment of young people. These include full-time education, the social services and the employment and training agencies, not to mention the media and various forms of commercial provision. The Youth Service is unique amongst them because its sole objective is the personal development of the individual.

3.8   Secondly, there is a need for experience not merely to be encountered but also to be, so to speak, taken into the system. By the "experiential" approach which we regard as characteristic of the Youth Service we mean that actual experience (rather than, say, theoretical or observed models) is used as the basis of a structured learning process. At this point we should be cautious. It may have been part of the conscious aims of some of the providers of services in the past to ensure that young people in their charge not merely encountered experience of the specific types mentioned above, but also recognised what they were encoun-

14

tering and drew the "right" lesson from it. But we must declare against such a one-way form of social control. It is no part of the Youth Service, as we see it, to be simply an instrument of cultural reproduction. We see the Youth Service as deeply educational, in the sense that it should be helping young people to become whatever it is in them to be. This means that the process of reflection and learning from experience must be open-ended and so far as possible self-directed. We conclude that the Youth Service must make it its business to provide the opportunity for reflection on experiences which it throws in the way of those who participate in it. The "experience of reflection", which is a kind of coping skill, can be added to the list given above; but this experience must follow a line freely chosen by the young participants themselves.

3.9 This leads to a final point, the recognition that young people need freedom to choose, to experiment and to reflect. The experiential need of one young person is different from that of another. Some may need to have their confidence restored, perhaps through exposure to the probably unfamiliar sensation of being valued for their own sake, before they can be in a position to grasp these freedoms. It should be the aim to bring these freedoms within the grasp of all; and this means that the Service is committed to variety of provision and to putting the young person in the position of both determining that variety and choosing from within it. In this way provision for young people's social education can be secured. We will enlarge upon these themes in later chapters. First, however, it will be useful to survey the current situation from the standpoint of the opportunities and types of experience which are available to young people apart from the Youth Service, and then the main types of Youth Service provision.

Other Institutions and Agencies

3.10 For the majority of young people *the family* is bound to be the prime provider of experience; and attitudes, emotions and ideas inside the family and the contacts that the family makes with the wider community will be the most potent factor in the young person's window on the world and interaction with it. Several factors have affected the nature of the family—such as the increase in numbers of single-parent families and the higher levels of divorce—but it still remains true that for most young people the family is seen as an important and stabilising force. In fact the survey of young people's opinions shows how for the majority of young people time spent in the home is appreciated more than any other. It cannot, however, always be relied upon as a sure fulfiller of the experiential needs noted in the last section. Concepts of personal valuation and the exchanging of ideas start from experience in the family, and any destructive experience there will be difficult to erase.

3.11 The *social environment* and network of relationships which constitutes society are sources of interpersonal experience for young people. We have talked (in 2.3) about the dramatic changes that have taken place in the neighbourhood, especially that of the inner-urban environment. There is more to be considered here than the more dramatic aspects of decay. In relatively newly created areas or those of high mobility the contact which the neighbourhood provides may not yet have had time to develop. In rural areas contacts with a wider range of the community may be more restricted than in the past because of the non-availability or prohibitively high cost of transport. High levels of unemployment (which may loom very large in restricted small communities) have a debilitating effect on the community's life and attitudes and on what it can provide and sustain in the way of facilities. Opportunities for working with other people are thus diminished.

3.12 An experience which will be common to all young people up to the age of 16 is *school*, and there are of course many opportunities here for the experiences which we see as necessary for development. Within the 16–19 age-range, only just over a quarter of the population attends full-time education at present, and the percentage is smaller in some areas. We have already mentioned that, for whatever reasons, young people do not always find the school process a fruitful or inspiring one, or make the contacts with adults that might be hoped for (though our survey showed that particularly on questions of careers young people frequently consider school staff among the more approachable adults). It is in any event unlikely that the development of the young person as a "whole person" will be totally encompassed by the life of the school. Some important experiences may be missing, in particular perhaps the experiences of freedom and self-determination.

3.13 Over a third of those in the 16–19 age-group in full-time education attend institutions of *further education*, and yet others take part-time courses in them. Further education may well be the focus of life for many of its students, and may encourage freer associations than at school, easier contacts with adults outside the family and more connections with the life of work. These, together with student union activities, may give the active young person plenty of scope for development. Nevertheless in general further education will often be seen as strictly functional or vocational. This may be more true of traditional further education courses than of some of the newer initiatives, including those linked with schemes funded by the Manpower Services Commission.

3.14 As we have seen in chapter 2, young people clearly feel that *being employed* is the most important factor on the road to becoming an adult. Apart from the possible responsibility of the job itself, the situation of being employed gives the young person the opportunity of most of the varieties of the experience mentioned above. In addition to the work itself, the facilities provided by some employers will themselves constitute a provision of leisure of a social kind which can bring satisfaction and enjoyment to the young employee. The absence of this experience of employment is correspondingly serious. Yet it has to be added that the mere possession of a job as such may not fulfil all the high hopes of the young people who aspire to adult status, especially if the work is narrow and unfulfilling, if there is no element of systematic vocational preparation, if the young person is conscious of being exploited as a cheap pair of hands, and especially if the tenure of the job is short-lived and insecure.

3.15 It is important to realise the essential difference between, and different needs resulting from, free time which is enforced by lack of employment and the free time enjoyed by young people in employment or education. Enforced free time will be begrudged and often accompanied by a lack of money. There is every reason for a negative view of society, and in many cases repeated failures to

16

obtain employment will have led to apathy and disillusion. A simple extension of the kind of leisure service that youth centres, leisure centres and to some extent youth clubs provide to a longer period of hours will not of itself answer the needs of those out of work. The true meaning of leisure can hardly exist outside the framework of work, and denying young people the possibility of work may in a sense also deprive them of the possibility of real leisure.

3.16 Experience for young people is also offered by *institutional networks* other than the Youth Service which are provided by central or local government. At the present time the *Manpower Services Commission* (MSC) is the foremost of these, both in the number of young people provided for and in the place it has in the public eye. We speak in chapters 6 (6.13—6.17) and 8 (8.38—8.39) about the proposed Youth Training Scheme (YTS), but apart from that the various programmes provided by the MSC have been for a number of years important elements in the lives of many young people. The involvement of the MSC in provision for young people goes back to the mid-70s. Earlier schemes of job creation were reviewed in 1976—77 in the Holland Report on 'Young People At Work', and this led to the setting up of the Youth Opportunities Programme (YOP) in 1978. Since that time the number of young people involved in the MSC's programmes has been steadily increasing. During the period we were working, the MSC initiated discussion on the New Training Initiative, an agenda for which was published in December 1981 at the same time as the Department of Employment's White Paper 'A New Training Initiative: A Programme for Action' (Cmnd. 8455). The Youth Task Group which was then set up produced its report in April 1982. It is envisaged that the new Youth Training Scheme scheduled to start in 1983 may embrace up to half a million young people.

3.17 In general all programmes provide some of the experiences of work together with input designed to develop skills, including personal skills, required for working life and adult life in general. Experiences currently offered to young people include work introduction, short training for special skills, longer courses offering work experience on employers' premises, and training workshops where technical skills and experience in making and selling products can be provided. Others can take part in community projects on which, with adult supervision, they can undertake work related to society. Remedial courses in colleges are available for some of the more disadvantaged young people. In addition to the experience inevitably provided by the activity on the skilled part of the course and by the environment where it takes place, all courses should include a specific element of training in social and life skills. Another scheme, intended for young people in employment, is Unified Vocational Preparation (UVP), again designed to improve skills for working life and adult life in general. UVP and YOP will be joined together and strengthened when the new Youth Training Scheme is brought into force. As we stress in chapter 6, the Youth Service plays a critical role in provision for the young unemployed in transition to working life. Community Industry was established by the National Association of Youth Clubs (NAYC) in 1970 before the creation of the MSC and, together with the 'Training for Life' programme of the Young Men's Christian Associations (YMCA), 'Springboard' promoted by Community Service Volunteers (CSV) and some local authority Youth and Community Services, it has remained a significant and distinctive aspect of MSC programmes.

17

3.18   There are other services, within the purview of the Department of Health and Social Security and the Home Office, which provide experience for young people in restricted categories. Local authorities provide various services stemming from the welfare provisions of Acts relating to children and young people. Apart from the provision for young people received into care or subject to care orders, provision is made under supervision orders which may well involve directions which require the participation of the young person in *Intermediate Treatment*. Young people designated "at risk" may also voluntarily be involved. Intermediate Treatment may be provided by special officers, social workers or probation officers, or may indeed be secured in co-operation with the Youth Service or voluntary organisations, the general aim being to prevent juvenile delinquency. A wide range of activities can be included in this provision—physical activities including sports, camping, vocational activity, guidance projects or fund-raising activities. Amounts and types of provision may vary widely from authority to authority so that the chance of a young person being involved in it varies according to locality.

3.19   *The probation and after-care service* works with those of 17 and over as a consequence of Probation Orders made by the Courts, in addition to its involvement in Intermediate Treatment mentioned in 3.18 above. With many of the young adults involved, it provides treatment and tries to secure rehabilitation in the community either via Community Service Orders or in a variety of schemes which provide both vocational preparation or training and recreational and social activities. These schemes are often organised in conjunction with the National Association for the Care and Resettlement of Offenders or with the social services or youth or adult education services of local authorities.

3.20   *Recreation and leisure-service* departments of local authorities, including district councils, also offer physical activities outdoors, or indoors in sports halls, swimming pools or other buildings, in much the same way as the Youth Service does. They make provision for most sports, nature trails, art, music and drama. For younger children, district councils may be major statutory providers and work with the Youth Service in joint use of staff or premises.

3.21   It is important not to overlook the amount of provision and experience for young people which exists outside the statutory or voluntary field. It falls broadly into two categories—the public house, café or commercial leisure centre which may attract a significant number of young people amongst its clientele; and the media in all their great variety—magazines, radio and television programmes, pop music and films, whether specially designed for young people or not. *The pub and other commercially sponsored forms of leisure-time provision* are important because they are part of the adult world and also provide scope for choice—for those young people who have the financial means to take advantage of it. In our survey they come higher on the list of ways of spending time than the Youth Service. Many of the youth workers to whom we spoke were strongly aware of this counter-attraction: its existence is one of the reasons why "detached" work (see 3.32 below) is a necessary complement to club provision. *The media* play a considerable part in structuring the time of young people. Many of the publications and programmes aimed directly at young people are excellent, and an important source of information and advice. But it is the

18

general impact of the media in their totality which is the more influential force. They are a powerful source of impressions and expectations, building and reinforcing the picture of the adult world to which young people aspire. They also mirror the confusion and perplexities of that world.

3.22 The overriding impression carried away by even the most casual observer of the whole scene is one of unco-ordinated development and change in those sectors which form part of the statutory or voluntary provision. Some influences or agencies are gaining in stength and importance, others are declining. There has been no attempt in recent times to look comprehensively at the total picture, and certainly no attempt by successive governments to make adjustments and allowances between even those parts over which they have partial control. There has up to now been little sign of any appropriate machinery to co-ordinate the policies being pursued by the social service departments and the Youth Service in most areas. This is a crucial point to which we shall return in subsequent chapters. (See 6.5−6.7 and 8.23−8.27.)

Types of Youth Service Provision Today

3.23 The present-day face of the Youth Service in England, as we have shown in chapter 1, is a varied and only partially integrated one. At all stages of its development institutions have been created in response to needs perceived by particular social, religious and quasi-political viewpoints, and many of these traditions still persist. We reserve until later a full critique of this scene: for the time being it is sufficient to outline the main types of provision.

3.24 The most common type of youth provision is some kind of club or local organisation which offers facilities for socialising and a basis for activities of various kinds. These local units may be organised in two main ways. On the one hand, there are large-scale movements on a national or international basis with a centralised organisation, providing the policy objectives and impetus for a large spread of local units, which may themselves have considerable autonomy of action within the policy guidelines. On the other hand, a large number of clubs owe their independent existence to some purely local initiative, often centred in a church, a community association or some other local charitable body, but have in the course of time become affiliated to a national organisation for purposes of mutual support.

3.25 The foremost representatives of the centralised type are the *uniformed organisations*, the Boys' and Girls' Brigades, the Scouts Association and the Girl Guides. These keep up their traditions of regularity of meetings, highly organised activity, fostering duty and obedience under the guidance of adult volunteer leaders, the incorporation of overt expressions of morality into their aims, and the wearing of uniforms. Virtually all of them have a distinctive hierarchy amongst both the young people and the adults, together with an outwardly rigid structure of objectives and traditions. It has to be noted, however, that these traditions have in general not prevented the organisations from responding to new and emerging needs often in quite radical ways, *e.g.* in the development of self-programming activities at local level. Moral and spiritual values are often emphasised through attachment to local churches; and international links are fostered. Programmes of activities, although, as mentioned above, usually a

19

matter for local decision, are generally based on developmental training schemes. A further source of strength is that adults may have a long history of identification with the organisation and with the local community. With the notable (and recent) exception of the Venture Scouts, the uniformed organisations are mostly single-sexed.

3.26 A specific group of uniformed organisations is that which offers activities based on aspects of the work of the armed forces. They are seen as providing, on an entirely voluntary basis, a programme of activities demanding a disciplined and ordered approach, but also giving opportunities for adventurous—mainly outdoor—activities on land and sea and in the air; the development of social, practical and technical skills; and the development of leadership and responsibility—sometimes involving forms of service to the community. Some parts of these cadet forces have recently moved away from being single-sexed.

3.27 The second type of organisation centres round the *local youth club*. The provision offered under this heading exhibits a huge variety in historical background, in style of operation, and in what is offered. The majority are voluntary organisations, many operating under church auspices, but a large number were provided by the local authority Youth Services in the post-Albemarle period. There is little difference between a statutory and a voluntary club. All normally meet in the evenings for a stated number of hours. The age-range may be wide or narrow, and particular nights may be reserved for particular age-groups, or reserved to one sex. Numbers may range from a few dozen to a few hundred. The general aim is to provide a place for the young people in a locality where they can meet, make friends, and spend their leisure time. Music, games and refreshment are normally provided: whether any more organised activity takes place will depend on the way the club is organised, which may change quite quickly over a period of time. Sport, cultural activities, discussions, outings, holidays, and community involvement may all be on the agenda from time to time. Within this setting the aim of most of these local organisations is to provide scope for social and political education, and for personal development of the members. Through their contacts with young people, adult workers (sometimes full-timers but more typically part-timers and volunteers) may offer opportunities for self-organisation, participation and group work, and for obtaining advice, information and personal counselling. It is clear that this endeavour makes great demands on the youth workers concerned.

3.28 We have seen great variety in the styles of leadership in the clubs we have visited. The range includes those where an authoritarian control is maintained, those where all decisions are taken by authority but the members' views are canvassed, those where the members have a limited but definite voice in the affairs of the club, and those where the running of the club is wholly or mainly in members' hands.

3.29 There are certain organisations, of which the Young Farmers' Clubs are the best known example, which are essentially local autonomous clubs but which have a clearly defined national structure on a representative basis. At all levels decisions are taken by members and their representatives.

3.30   The distinction between a youth club and a *youth centre* is sometimes hard to draw. In general youth centres, which have often developed from junior evening institutes, put more emphasis on the specific activities which they provide and less on the social side, though rooms for refreshment and informal activities are usually provided. They are often located on or near a school site and share some of the school facilities. If so, those using the centre may tend to be drawn predominantly from the school concerned, but this need not be so. While physical activities are the main ingredient, art, craft, music, drama and language classes may well also be offered. Instruction in special areas may be provided when required. Centres are generally run by a warden, with tutors provided for the various activities. Members here are primarily concerned with the activities, as opposed to clubs where there is a concern for the whole institution. One concept of centre provision is that of 'excellence', since the provision is seen as the central resource for an area to make the most use of specialist facilities. As a result young people from other clubs and organisations can use the facilities to develop their activity skills to higher levels.

3.31   A wide range of organisations has been established in a number of areas to focus on matters of local interest. They may be *youth parliaments, local youth councils or forums, or young adult groups*, which will differ from most other youth provision because they will be organised and run by young people for other young people. In many cases these will have been set up by young people themselves, usually with assistance from local youth or voluntary associations. They will vary greatly in membership but may include young people drawn from local groups of the national voluntary youth organisations, statutory youth clubs or community-based groups and from young political and student groups. Activities may include organising competitions, social and recreational events and fund-raising for charities, but the chief purpose of such organisations is normally to focus the attention of young people on matters of a political nature in the local community with efforts directed to some sort of action as well as discussion. This is an important strand in youth provision which we shall be considering in some detail in chapter 5.

3.32   *Detached work*, developed especially in the years post-Albemarle for young people who are "unattached", tends to be concentrated in inner cities or in other areas where there is a high mobility of the young population and a lack of fixed provision. There is a wide variety in what is offered but important considerations are that a project should have a specific "target group" of young people which is limited in size. Work may lead to the establishment of a particular group or fixed base for young people's use. Workers may be based on existing provision, or work from particular premises, such as coffee bars or Open Door clubs, which have no concept of membership and can attract "unattached" young people. This kind of provision is normally very closely related to the area. The great majority of authorities employ workers designated as detached.

3.33   One function of detached projects may be to offer *counselling* to young people, but there is in addition a wide variety of specialist organisations engaged in offering both advice and counselling which have sprung up particularly since the 1960s. Changes in society have brought about a need for adult advice both on personal matters and on specific problems such as unemployment, homelessness, sexual and legal matters. Agencies to deal with such matters may be statutory or voluntary, and again there is a wide variety of style in the type of provision offered, related both to the function of the organisation and its philosophy. Sessions for individuals or groups may take place inside an institution with a worker on the normal staff of that institution, or with a visiting worker, or may be part of a special project.

3.34 Various types of *community provision* have developed, especially in the last decade. The term "youth and community" is elastic, and is used to describe a number of different kinds of provision. Community centres exist to provide a wide range of opportunity to the community they serve, in the arts, in matters of local interest or in other activities. Youth work may well be involved in this provision either integrally or separately. Some areas employ community workers to promote activity in many directions in the local community. They may work on housing estates or developments in order to encourage community feeling or expression, and similar work may be done in particularly rundown areas. Again work with young people may well be involved. Another particular type of community provision is community schools. These are organised in a number of different ways, but the aim of most of them is to bring together the work of the school and the community. This sometimes involves secondary schools where some classes may be attended by adults, and classes in the evenings can be attended by students at the school. Normally the organisation itself is in some way integrated: it is not simply a question of joint use of facilities or premises, as with youth centres. Work of a similar nature may be carried out in schools not specifically designated community schools.

3.35 *Play provision* for the lower age-range of young people has the same general aims of experience and social education in an educational context as youth provision for other age-groups, but particular types of provision are appropriate. Play centres offer creative play provision for younger members and are often extended into junior clubs which provide a version of the youth club or centre for these members. Instruction, coaching and supervision are provided, and freedom of expression is encouraged along with experiential learning. During holiday periods play schemes providing a range of social provision and activities are organised over an extended period. Adventure playgrounds may also be part of the junior youth organisation: they offer a protected area in the community within which young people can indulge in challenging and even dangerous activities with a safety net of skilled supervision.

3.36 The types of provision described so far account for the standard range of services which are expected to be found in any area, but providers, both statutory and voluntary, have recognised the need for extensions of the Service beyond what can be provided in an area or in the normal range of activities of young people within the usual spans of time and the usual constraints of space. To provide fully extended provision, other styles of working are necessary. Thus *residential centres* have been established to provide a wide variety of courses for young people and training courses for those who work with them. Courses for young people may be run at weekends, for a week or for several weeks: they may be offered by the centre or run by outside youth agencies, schools or colleges. They can be open invitation courses or closed courses for particular youth organisations or groups, and most place great emphasis on the use and importance of residential experience for adolescents as well as on the particular specialist aspect of the course. This may include personal development, school-to-work courses, courses for young workers, creative or expressive courses, Youth Opportunities Programme projects, activities organised through youth councils, or environmental education activities. Residential centres have an important integrating function in emphasising unity over an area, whether county, regional or national, or in respect of a specialist activity with which the centre has become identified. Another method of extending the range of possibilities available to a young person is offered by specially set up outdoor-pursuit centres, either within the boundaries of an authority or elsewhere, often in physically challenging situations. In the years following Albemarle there was considerable development of this type of provision by local authorities and national specialist outdoor-pursuits organisations.

3.37   A number of centres are also to be found which specialise in other directions. Obvious examples are arts projects, youth theatres, music groups, cruises and centres associated with particular sporting interests such as fishing or motorbikes. In some cases these *specialist activities* have given rise to specific organisations. Centres also have an important role in training.

3.38   Over the last two decades a number of organisations have come into being to encourage various forms of *community service* or community involvement. This is an important development which has taken place partly inside Youth Service organisations but partly also separately and outside them. Some of the organisations have a national or regional structure but a number are locally based to provide opportunities for young people to undertake work with those in need in their localities, whether individuals, institutions or the communities themselves. Some have an environmental slant. Many schemes are organised by or work in co-operation with schools. Others offer clearing houses for young people and jobs, prepare volunteers for their work and help them to understand the experience they undergo. Some are organised by young people themselves. We shall be referring to this type of provision in some detail in chapter 5.

3.39   There exists an important and varied group of organisations, both national and local, which cater for the specialised and often sophisticated interests, aptitudes and concerns of young people and have attracted considerable numbers. The range is wide, including outdoor activities, environmental and development education groups and the arts. The varying activities are often seen as a conscious instrument of social education and, where a skill element is involved, high quality performance is expected.

3.40   *The Duke of Edinburgh's Award* is a special scheme which, by liaison with other organisations and contact with individuals, gives young people the chance to gain an award by meeting certain standards in service to the community, adventurous expedition, development of personal skills or participation in physical recreation. It covers many young people in school as well as those in the Youth Service and reaches many who are not otherwise involved in any youth organisation. It also provides a vehicle for non-specialist youth clubs or organisations to tackle a more sophisticated range of interests in their own programmes.

3.41   In addition to the types of organisation mentioned so far, which are provided specifically for young people, there are organisations which address the population at large but find it desirable and useful to make special arrangements to involve their younger members. The *churches* have a long-established tradition of sponsoring youth clubs and uniformed groups, but their provision for young people does not stop there. Some young people value association with youth fellowship groups, whose programmes are based on spiritual and religious affairs but may include a wide range of social and political issues and activities. Often two or three different types of provision are associated with one congregation.

3.42   Many young people especially in the older age-range are involved in the youth wings of the *political parties*. On some issues these youth wings may have different views from their parent bodies, although they are part of the party structure. They organise activities of a purely political nature including election-campaigning and lobbying, but in many cases they also provide social and recreational activities and an opportunity for young people to participate in assemblies and conferences.

3.43   We have recently seen the development of a range of *co-ordinating agencies* in the Youth Service. Organisations like the National Council for Voluntary Youth Services and the British Youth Council have played a crucial role in attempting to co-ordinate the policies and practices of the many different youth organisations. In addition to this the machinery of the All-Party Parliamentary Youth Affairs Lobby has given youth organisations and young people an opportunity to present their case directly to Members of Parliament, and this has assisted in placing youth affairs issues on the political agenda.

3.44   We have left to the end mention of *handicapped* young people in order to avoid giving the impression that specialist provision is always necessary for them. Many handicapped young people are to be found taking part in the day-to-day work of clubs, centres and organisations of every kind. Some do, however, require a specialist type of organisation, and we shall be dealing with these in a specific section in chapter 6.

Conclusion to Part I

3.45   At the conclusion of this factual and analytical part of our report, and before we move to an appraisal of needs and how they are met, it seems worthwhile recapitulating some of the good and bad aspects of present provision.

3.46   On the good side, we have to note both the immense variety of provision for young people and the fertility of new ideas within the various agencies at work in the field. The Youth Service with its varied heritage of approaches and traditions includes features which are crucially relevant to the situation of young people today, in particular the tradition of voluntaryism, the emphasis on personal relationships, and the idea of active participation by young people themselves in working out their own provision. These are themes which we shall develop further.

3.47 On the debit side, the impact of all this provision is confusing because the various agencies at work in the field tend to develop their policies and practices and employ their resources in almost total isolation from each other. There is a need to put together, at local and national level, a more concerted strategy. We must also note that the good intentions which have inspired much of what is provided are not always followed up in performance. For example, despite repeated calls for participation by young people in running their own activities, progress in this direction has been slow. Standards of provision in general are very uneven, and most important of all the network remains incomplete, so that some of those young people who most need social education are still not reached by it. We shall examine these matters in more detail in chapter 5.

PART 2   ASSESSMENT AND PROGNOSIS

CHAPTER 4:   VIEWS OF THE YOUTH SERVICE IN SUBMISSIONS TO THE REVIEW GROUP

The opinions voiced to the Group by local authorities, voluntary organisations, local groups and individuals. General agreement over aims of the Youth Service; positive and negative features of the Service. Views on workers, clubs, projects; partnership between the statutory and voluntary sector; and training. Rejection of the idea of compulsory voluntary service. Views on provision in rural areas. Priorities for the Service and the ages with which it should be concerned. Some views held by young people.

4.1   In this part we begin to develop and explain our views on the Youth Service; but we cannot do so without first paying tribute to the quality and quantity of written response to the lists of questions which we sent out. Nearly every local education authority, many district councils, all the large national voluntary organisations and most training agencies sent submissions. Many not only gave detailed and lengthy responses to the questions we asked, but also included papers, research reports, pamphlets and books which had been produced in the course of their work, and set out views and evidence on a range of topics relevant to young people. Frequently local authorities and others had circulated copies of our questions to individuals involved in youth work, and used their responses as a basis for a general reply or included them as an annex to a central response. We also received many letters and responses from individuals—young people, workers, officers and people with long experience in voluntary youth work.

4.2   All this has been supplemented by contacts we have made during visits to clubs and centres and through specially convened meetings of authorities' staff and voluntary organisations in various parts of the country. A number of national oganisations representing voluntary services, officers and other interests have also given us their opinions in meetings of the Group. We have taken special pains to listen to the views of young people, through meetings arranged locally, through arrangements made nationally and through phone-in and other radio programmes.

4.3   This has been useful in various ways. It has included a vast amount of factual information on resources, staffing arrangements and young people which has been invaluable in our consideration of resources and the deployment of the Service. Further, the deeply considered comment made by those with long experience in the field has informed our thinking on all the issues which make up the substance of the report. Many submissions suggested ways of approach and gave insights which were vital in shaping our conclusions.

4.4   In the following paragraphs we indicate the range and direction of views given in evidence, point out the areas of concern, and mention some particular opinions on specific issues on which we give our own views in later chapters.

4.5   Many submissions commented widely on the *current situation of youth*, as we have done in chapter 2. Changes in the relationship between young people, their parents and authority in general were constantly mentioned; and it was widely felt that there was an increasing pressure on young people—and therefore on the Youth Service—particularly as a result of unemployment.

4.6   Two notable features about the responses were the considerable thought which all had clearly given to general questions involving the Service, and a remarkable unanimity about the *aims and philosophy* of the Service, in contrast to the variety of opinion held about its *performance*.

4.7   Virtually all respondents saw the Youth Service as an educational one. While the term social education was not usually defined, the aim of the process was clearly seen as helping the young person on the path to maturity, with participation in leisure-time activity as the main agent. The importance of the concept "community involvement" was often stressed in this context. The orientation of the Service towards the community was felt to be especially necessary at the present time; and "participation", though rarely described or defined, was considered to give young people greater awareness of the community. The help that the Service could give in developing a young person's personal life was stressed: it could provide a stable reference point during the period in growth when it was particularly necessary to have one; and the additional concept of "challenge" was something the Youth Service especially could provide. These general developmental concepts were suggested far more frequently than specific skills or programmes, though the Service was often felt to have a role in developing physical co-ordination and personal skills.

4.8   Respondents claimed for the Service a number of positive features which could help it to achieve these aims. Undoubtedly the strongest of these was the work-force itself: in addition to the dedication of workers, the wide variety in their background and experience was an enormous asset. The Youth Service had some other advantages which other services could not boast: its traditions allowed the young person to be considered as an individual, and its diversity and relative freedom of organisation gave it a potential dynamism and sensitivity to the immediate needs of the local community or neighbourhood.

4.9   Despite these strengths at an individual and local level, however, there was a general feeling that the Service was not achieving as much as it could and should. The reasons given for this fell into two main types—those connected with resources and those connected with the organisation of the Service.

4.10   On the one hand, most submissions considered that resources were inadequate. Even if financial resources had not fallen, the view was that they had not kept pace with the large number of new demands on the Service; that the lack of a statutory base for the Service made it especially vulnerable; and that there was a particular risk in the immediate future of cuts in the Service. Training programmes, staff numbers and project work were thought to be especially threatened.

4.11   On the other hand, it was frequently stated that a lack of cohesion and sense of direction in the Service prevented the resources which were available from being used to the greatest advantage. The fact that many sources of funds were involved made the matter no easier. Despite the general agreement on aims mentioned above, there was an almost equally general feeling that the Service, when it came to the point, did not have any overall policy or sense of direction. Some aspects were described as conservative—slow to adapt to changes in society, and all too often concerned with petty rivalry, buildings or numbers rather than social matters, which should be the overriding objective. The existence of a wide variety of types of provision, of full-time, part-time and volunteer workers, and of both statutory and voluntary sectors was in itself an advantage, but co-ordination between them was generally seen as inadequate. The result was that the Service lacked cohesion and was sometimes at odds with itself, uneven in quality and response to demand, and was not in a position to marshal its forces to acquire a coherent voice in promoting an understanding of its aims in the general public or in acquiring resources. Some respondents suggested that on occasions the Service would try to respond to demand without assessing its ability to do so: continuous agreement to new demands weakened the existing provision and left workers uncertain about where the centre of concern should be. A major reason for this was felt by some to be that officers had in a relatively few cases had professional training in the Youth Service; and, particularly in evidence to us by voluntary organisations, there was a feeling that the statutory sector did not have sufficient understanding of what the voluntary could achieve. More paid staff to work in the voluntary sector was suggested as one way of helping this.

4.12   It was also suggested that links with other providers of services for young people, such as schools, further education, social services and probation services, were weak or non-existent.

4.13   The view of the *"ideal worker"* was again a matter of general agreement. All the many descriptions fitted in with the view of the aim of the Service as providing social education. Attributes suggested emphasised the need for responsibility, approachability and flexibility, which would ensure a good relationship with young people and would enable workers to remain confident when the situation became difficult and work had to be done under pressure.

4.14   While some respondents stressed the need for the Youth Service to develop and diversify the traditional approach typified by the *club*, there is no doubt that most still saw the club as the most important element of the Service. The security, social structure and manageable size of a club, whether a new or an established one, made it ideal for some kinds of work. There were also pointers to the kinds of problems that could go with the running of a club: a feeling of smugness, an unwillingness to be outgoing, a readiness to accept things as they were and to keep on the same activities. These activities, often fairly traditional in nature, could too easily become the be-all-and-end-all of a club's existence, and a reasonable showing of attendance could too readily be taken as proof that a club was doing its job. Some suggested that young people themselves were too ready to accept this and not active enough in taking on responsibility for deciding and organising what the club should do. Yet young people (as we explain in 4.27) felt that they were being denied the opportunity to play an active role. It was often said that, in addition to providing social education and organising activities, which were themselves one of the main channels of social education, a club should direct young people's attention outwards by encouraging participation in community activities and by developing young people's political awareness of wider issues and readiness to take action if necessary.

4.15   Many respondents gave details of *projects* they were undertaking and how these had affected their community. They demonstrated awareness of particular needs—some resulting from poor provision and social circumstances, some to be found among groups of young people not using clubs who could nevertheless benefit from provision—and the energetic and imaginative ways people were evolving of coming to grips with them. Experience had shown, all the same, some of the dangers inherent in this type of work. Initial enthusiasm could flag, and financial or other help given by organisations could dry up before the project was completed. The lack of commonly accepted indicators of success could cause questions to be asked which put promoters and workers in a vulnerable position. Target groups and expectations might be unrealistically high. Despite these risks, it was widely believed that, given proper planning, monitoring and management, project work should be an expanding arena for the Service. Organisations submitted several papers and publications suggesting ways in which efficient management of projects could be achieved.

4.16   Many submissions gave views on the traditional *partnership between statutory and voluntary sectors*. It was acknowledged that in many cases contacts and co-operation took place, both formally and informally, and matters of concern were discussed amicably and constructively. Details were provided of the structures developed, sometimes over many years, to encompass partnership. In areas where no formal arrangements existed, voluntary organisations in particular made it clear that they would like to see them. More generally, however, there was a feeling that, under the increasing pressure on the Youth Service, such partnership needed to be made to work better. Not unnaturally, the emphases of voluntary and statutory correspondents were a little different, each side sometimes feeling the other did not properly appreciate the work they were doing. Many authorities gave voluntary bodies representation on the committees which took decisions or gave advice about youth provision. It was generally felt that this should always happen and that, whatever particular structure was appropriate, no decisions should be taken about youth work provision without both sides having a systematic opportunity to make an input.

4.17   While some local authorities felt that *current arrangements for training* were adequate, many other respondents raised doubts. Their criticism was fairly uniform. It was mostly concerned with the training needs of full-time staff. By far the most frequently stated comment was the need to make more provision for management and administrative skills in training programmes. It was felt the training should be more "practical" and should encourage students to recognise realities. A number of responses mentioned that there should be more liaison on a regular basis between the field and the various agencies which trained full-time staff. There were comments, too, that assessment of students should be based more on field-work, given that the greater part of current provision was still premises-based; and that students should be aware of the traditional role of the Service. Placements in training should also reflect the precise type of work that students were likely to take up and the areas in which they were likely to do it, although it was necesary for them to have knowledge of other localities as well.

29

Occasionally there was criticism that the content of courses was too student-directed, though more often the personal development of the student was seen as of basic importance. It was felt that there was no overall standard for acceptance of students on courses.

4.18   Many submissions suggested a three-year course should be the norm: this would give the youth worker equal professional status with teachers and social workers. Courses should preferably lead to qualifications, or the possibility of later gaining qualifications, for other careers; or at least some element of common training should be provided. It was also considered that the present situation by which a qualified teacher was automatically accepted as qualified for youth work was unsatisfactory. Respondents were also greatly concerned that grants for students accepted on full-time youth work courses were not mandatory.

4.19   Submissions suggested that there should be more training opportunities for part-time staff and that they should be of a practical nature. The single most mentioned requirement was for national standards for part-time workers and, related to that, agreed national scales of payment. It was important that there should be facilities, for those who wished, to study part-time to gain higher qualifications, and there was a general need to have courses above basic level.

4.20   A significant body of criticism reached us from *professional associations* in the Youth Service. One association spoke especially strongly of a need for special training for those appointed to officer posts. Many who were now in such positions had started work in the Youth Service before existing courses were developed, or had transferred from other areas. Proper training in professional and management skills was necessary if officers were to have confidence both in dealing with their work-force and in promoting the cause of youth work to those in authority. It was essential that there should be a strong professional voice to promote the Youth Service in education authorities.

4.21   Professional bodies also suggested a need for more effective liaison with training agencies and the creation of a structure to monitor their provision, in order not only to ensure the best training for full-time staff, but also to bring about a properly considered national policy of recruitment carried out according to national and special needs. Qualifications to enter courses should be consistent and on a par with similar courses; and a longer period of training would be an advantage. The arrangement giving qualfied teachers qualified youth worker status should be reviewed: most professional associations felt that it should be brought to an end. All these changes in the system would help to give the Service a higher professional standing and image.

4.22   In-service training programmes, especially for part-time staff, needed to be rigorously implemented. Attention was drawn to current difficulties in attracting staff to such courses—particularly in rural areas, where the unwillingness or inability of authorities to pay expenses made attendance prohibitive. It was suggested that schemes which some authorities had in the past been organising jointly with others were now less frequent.

4.23   Many of the submissions mentioned the topic of *community service* and schemes of a national kind for providing it. We also spoke to representatives of some organisations promoting such schemes. All were agreed on the developmental value of such work for young people, and felt that opportunities should be expanded and young people encouraged to take part, both on a part-time and a full-time basis. It was stressed that developmental needs of young people, rather than the community's needs, should be the criterion for judging such schemes, though some respondents felt there was no conflict between the two. While a national system to plan schemes might be useful, the strong general feeling was that local schemes were best. These should be planned and organised by people who knew the area, who had sufficient experience to recognise the planning problems, and who could ensure that young people derived the greatest educational value. There had been talk of compulsory schemes of community service, but virtually all respondents (including some representatives of the organisation 'Youth Call') opposed compulsion, since it would destroy one of the main elements of community service, namely that it should be freely chosen by young people themselves.

4.24   Several submissions from *rural areas* and some others stressed the need for provision for young people in such areas. It was felt that a special rural programme was as necessary as special help for urban areas. Isolation and the decline of public transport in country areas all led to disadvantage, and yet expenditure on the Service here appeared to be much lower. Current calculations of central government grant did not allow sufficient weighting to take account of the high cost of provision in rural areas. Efforts needed to be put into researching the needs of rurally based young people and providing for them.

4.25   There was some reluctance to specify any areas of work to be given *priority*, since respondents felt this might draw attention away from the important task of maintaining the work that was presently being done. Nearly all mentioned, however, the particular needs created by unemployment, especially for those young people who had just left school. Of those respondents who specified further areas for priority, many felt that in particular counselling services should be improved and increased, and that in many areas there was a need for more detached work, along with recognition by authorities of both its necessity and its achievements. Many submssions drew attention to the problem of the young and single homeless. It seemed that youth workers were frequently involved in finding short-term solutions to housing crises; and the shortage of accommodation available for young single people forced many of them to remain in the family home, in some cases causing conflict.

4.26   While there was some variety in what authorities felt should be the priority *age-range* for youth work, most submissions suggested it should start around 11 and finish about 20. Some felt that the younger age-group in particular could be catered for by voluntary organisations, though the voluntary organisations themselves did not suggest this. While one or two other submissions argued that the main age-group to which resources should be directed should be the younger group, since work here would forestall development of disruptive behaviour at later ages, most felt the years just before and after the minimum school-leaving age were the ones for maximum attention.

4.27   In our discussions with *young people* we found they were especially concerned with the general context of their lives and the need for their views about how society was run to be taken seriously. They wanted to have an effective say in the running of organisations and in other decisions concerned with their welfare. They did not accept the claim sometimes advanced that giving young people decision-making authority did not work, and even that young people themselves did not want it; but felt that even those who claimed to believe in young people's right to make decisions were sometimes unwilling to accept the implications of this when decisions were actually made. Having representatives of young people on committees could too easily be mere tokenism. Conferences of young people were organised by some bodies, but resolutions made at them might not be accepted by a parent organisation when it came to the point.

4.28   Young people gave views on the nature of Youth Service provision. While some felt that there was too much emphasis on sports and activities at present, others were quite happy with this balance. Many were concerned about suggestions that there might be a system of compulsory community service, as referred to in 4.23 above, and made clear their opposition to any such schemes.

4.29   Unemployment was naturally a concern of all the young people we met. Many felt the education system did not prepare young people for a future which included the likelihood of unemployment. Several reported unfortunate experiences in Youth Opportunities Programmes (YOP) schemes: some felt that they had been exploited. For many, however, the experience had been extremely useful.

4.30   There was one other point, made not only by young people but also by many officers and workers in both statutory and voluntary sectors. This concerned the financial position of young people. Some had an income from their jobs, though they might not be receiving any training; some were receiving a smaller income from the YOP allowance, but were receiving training; others, who had opted to stay in full-time education, often in order to improve their employability, were largely getting nothing. This anomaly was considered illogical and burdensome.

CHAPTER 5: CRITICAL APPRAISAL OF THE YOUTH SERVICE

The Group's views on current Youth Service theory and practice; its potential and actual performance; centre-based and project-based work. Some important modes of operation—participation in decision-making, counselling, community involvement, political education, international aspects.

5.1   In this chapter we shall be developing and explaining our own views on what the Youth Service is doing and should be doing to carry out its primary function of meeting, along with other agencies, the developmental needs of young people. We must make clear at the outset our acceptance and endorsement of the view, cogently argued by many organisations with long and wide experience in the youth field, such as the National Association of Youth Clubs, and backed by much research, that youth is *not* a time of continuous crisis—a sort of developmental disaster area. Of course all young people have problems as they grow up, but large numbers of young people cope with them successfully, with the help of parents, relatives, friends and their own peer group which has customarily been available in all kinds of society. Although there are forces at work in our society which tend to make these problems very difficult for some, it remains true—and our opinion survey confirms this—that the majority of young people are not in a state of crisis. Nevertheless, the message conveyed by the history of the youth movement to date is that the process of personal development is never easy, and that for a significant and probably increasing minority the process is, through no fault of the young people concerned, desperately difficult.

5.2   Faced with the wide spectrum of needs, we must state as a first principle that the Youth Service has the opportunity and the duty to help all young people who have need of it. While to some young people the Service may appear simply as a means of pleasurably extending their experience, to others it may be a real rescue service. It is important, in our view, that it continue to fulfil both these purposes, and not to concentrate on one to the exclusion of the other. It can sustain both roles, because the methods, context and person-to-person relationships on which the Service is based are flexible enough to fit it for both normal and crisis situations.

The Potential Role

5.3   It is precisely this feature which makes the Service potentially one of the most significant vehicles of social education. In chapter 3 we identified experience as the most meaningful factor in the process of social education. The right "mix" of experience for any particular individual cannot be prescribed. Opportunities can be provided, but the very act of choosing amongst them argues a certain degree of maturity: some young people need help merely to reach this point.

5.4   One can discern here the beginnings of both a beneficent and a vicious spiral. Where opportunities for experience of the right sort are available, and the young have the confidence or the encouragement to grasp them and to know what they are grasping, personal development follows. Where these opportunities are denied, the very confidence to exercise choice may wither, and alienation may result, brought about by extremes of frustration and despair.

5.5   The Youth Service is not of course the only agency seeking to reinforce the upward spiral and to arrest or reverse the downward one, but it has developed methods and resources *specifically* adapted to these needs. Foremost amongst these are:

(1) *The experiential curriculum:* The Youth Service, as we have found, believes strongly in its educational role, with emphasis on the principle of "learning by doing". The process is one which starts with experience and leads through reflection to further experience, such experience being as we have said of the widest kind and essentially self-programmed.

(2) *Participation in decision-making:* Through the Youth Service young people may for the first time gain experience of what it means to take and follow through collective decisions, and to direct their own activity along with others in an effective and responsible way.

(3) *Voluntaryism* both in membership and to a large extent in the adult worker role: It is of the essence of the Youth Service that young people remain free to participate or not as they choose. Any form of compulsion destroys this essence. It is also a significant feature of the Service that a large part of its workforce are part-timers or volunteers. We shall have more to say about this in chapter 9. Here we simply note that this involvement of people from all walks of life strongly reinforces the experiential nature of the social education process which the Youth Service can offer.

(4) *A non-directive relationship between workers and young people:* This follows from the other features. Youth workers have of course a certain authority, but their authority has to be of a different kind from that which young people are likely to have experienced from their teachers, parents and other caring (and non-caring) adults. In brief, young people find with the right sort of youth worker that their views and attitudes are treated with respect.

5.6   All these features can be, often have been, and certainly should be brought into full play in those modes of operation which the public are most apt to see as typical of the Youth Service, namely the youth club or youth organisation with its emphasis on corporate identity and a programme of activities. As we have seen, these modes have in the past constituted the core of Youth Service provision, and they will surely continue to be a prominent part of it. Even within these modes, however, few organisers would argue that mere association or mere activity was all that was being offered. Other ingredients must be present, and these can be offered outside the club setting, in a more specialised form. It is this very variety of form which makes the Youth Service such a potentially powerful force in responding to various categories of need.

Actual Performance

5.7   It has to be said that at the present time this potential is only partly being realised and that as a result the Youth Service is not meeting the social education

34

needs of young people as fully as it could. We must consider the reasons for this, but it is important to recognise that any criticism along these lines is in point only because the Youth Service has shown by its very success over the years that it is capable of much more. All parties have contributed to this success. Voluntary bodies have shown great flexibility while remaining true to the spirit of their founders. Local education authorities have shown remarkable staying power, often in the face of severe financial difficulties, in continuing to follow up in spirit and in resource terms the lead given long ago in Circular 1486; and have often rivalled the voluntary bodies in inventiveness. By the same token we think all share in the root causes of the failure to obtain the full promise of the Service.

5.8   There are no doubt many who would argue that this failure is basically attributable to a lack of resources. This may be a contributory factor, since nobody can truthfully say that money has been thrown at the Youth Service. We shall be considering the record in chapter 10. Here we would simply observe that in our view the causes of the failure to achieve full promise go deeper than just the resourcing of the Youth Service. As nearly as we can make out, the basic factors are the following:

(1) A failure to work out a coherent and generally accepted theory of social education. Responsibility for this lies at the national level as much as or more than at the local level: there are no instruments for the formulation of accepted objectives.

(2) A failure to put across the meaning and importance of social education. This may sound surprising when the literature of the youth movement is full of argument about the term. But there is a lack of consensus which would register with local councillors, Members of Parliament and the public. Generally speaking the public just does not know what the Youth Service is about.

(3) A patchy and incomplete response to newly emerging social needs. Some parts of the Youth Service are quick to perceive and react to new situations, but in others the responses are very slow and arbitrary, or alternatively take place to the detriment of existing provision.

(4) A failure to appreciate the value and purpose of all the tools which lie ready to hand, to keep proper balance between them and to proportion them to the tasks in hand, which vary from area to area and from time to time. There are many fads and fancies in the youth movement, rarely a balanced strategy.

(5) A failure to exploit all the methods fully. Resources do play a big part here. Initiatives are started without proper evaluation and then not adequately monitored. They may then wane for lack of support even if successful. The strategy and funding should be consistent and long-term, and subject to evaluation.

(6) A failure to take relations with the local community seriously. This again may seem surprising in view of the professed purposes of many youth and community departments. But we have found that community liaison is often more honoured in the breach than the observance. Sometimes the very impetus towards a comprehensive strategy destroys responsiveness to small but important community groups.

(7) A failure to maintain liaison with other providers of services cognate with the Youth Service.

(8) Insufficient scope for young people to organise or share in the organisation of their own activities, or be fully involved in the running of the Youth Service.

(9) Inadequate provision to meet the needs of the over-16s.

5.9 Nearly all these factors are aspects of management or training. They are not of course uniform and universal. Some LEAs and voluntary bodies have shown what can be done, but there is a big gap between these and the generality. We shall have more to say about management in chapter 8. We now propose to illustrate what we say by referring to certain key types of provision.

Centre-based and Project-Based Work

Clubs

5.10 We have seen some excellent clubs and some bad ones. Where they are good, it seems most often to be the case that the organisers, whether statutory or voluntary, have succeeded, first, in maintaining links with the local community and, secondly, in encouraging in various ways the full participation of the members. Success is to be measured not in the sheer number of people participating—though it will usually be found that a club which is successful in other ways does tend to attract large numbers—but in the satisfaction that they get out of it, in the scope that they have for taking decisions of their own about it, in the range, variety and freshness of the activities undertaken, in the numbers of part-time staff and volunteers who take part, and, less tangibly perhaps, in the extent to which members are helped and help each other with counsel and support. Lack of success means the opposite of these things: stereotyped activities, bored and haphazard membership, poor adult support, no real link with the locality.

5.11 Paradoxically club provision, often regarded as the mainstream of youth provision, is in some ways rather a neglected area. Development grants have often tended to be directed to experimental work and not to investigation of the factors making for success in clubs. It is clear that leadership plays a large part in this situation. For example, participation—a feature to which we shall devote a later section of this chapter (5.17–5.22)—is very much dependent on a worker's personal style, skill and commitment. But a worker needs good support, in the shape of premises, equipment, a reasonable allotment of part-time hours, and also a management committee composed of committed people from the neighbourhood. These are matters for the providing body to attend to, and not all do this. Quite often, for example, premises are quite disgracefully tatty, as though anything would do for a youth club.

5.12 One matter which clearly does lie within the competence of providing authorities, whether statutory or voluntary, is the geographical distribution of clubs and centres. Time and again in the course of our visits we have found gross inequalities in the incidence of provision. Areas of a city which are by no means the worst off in terms of facilities will be found to be relatively well endowed with

36

youth provision by comparison with, say, outlying housing estates which have little or none. There could be an opportunity nowadays, when educational premises are becoming vacant, to alter this situation. We are conscious of the constraints but we still think that something could be done to make sure that the new youth provision is where it is needed, either by the local authorities themselves or by arrangement with a voluntary body. Some of this is going on, but not enough. It is clear that in some cases, whatever arrangements exist, partnership is not working and the overall distribution of resources is not thought out.

5.13   We are aware that in some youth clubs and centres there can be a conflict between providing a wide range of activities and achieving personal development. It is a priority that the staffing of any particular centre should be adequate to meet the individual needs of the participants. Whilst the use of specialists may mean that a wide choice of programme is available, and some specialists become involved in far more of the life of the club than just their own activity, a concentration on specialist staff may prevent the club from meeting the developmental needs of its members. Another dilemma lies in finding the best programme and style for members after the age of 16; they may sometimes feel at this age that the range of activities provided by the club is no longer for them. Our survey indicated boredom at this stage. Self-programming provision is particularly successful here and more attention to the particular needs of the age-group is an urgent requirement.

Uniformed Organisations

5.14   We have referred above (in 3.25–3.26) to the particular contribution of the uniformed organisations. Between them the Girl Guides and Scouts, Girls' and Boys' Brigades and other such groups are the choice of a large number of young people, especially in the younger age-groups. We are impressed by the way in which they have endeavoured to revise their programmes and structures to meet the current needs of their members and yet remain true to their original aims. There are, however, two concerns. A long history of identification with an organisation by some adults is a real source of strength but can also inhibit openness to new ideas. Secondly, the size and history of the uniformed groups can separate them from the rest of the Youth Service. We would encourage them to develop closer links with other providers from whom they can learn and whose work they can enrich.

Project Work

5.15   Albemarle gave some encouragement to complementary work with the "unattached", and in both the LEA and voluntary sectors a number of initiatives have developed in so-called detached or project work. Neither term is particularly apt. The former, which usually connotes work with young people undertaken by full-time and part-time staff on the streets, in coffee bars and other places where the young people might gather, is negative (implying that the young people "ought" to be in a club) and seems to carry overtones of lack of accountability and weak or non-existent management controls. The latter term "project" is usually associated with experimental but nonetheless planned ventures such as advice centres, drop-in centres, employment schemes and the

37

like, which are not associated with a corporate organisation such as a club. We prefer to use the term project-based in an extended sense to mean all work which is not based on a club or centre with a definite membership. It does not mean an absence of buildings, since most project work requires some kind of base, if only an office; and it most definitely does not imply an absence of appropriate structures for management and supervision.

5.16   In fact, project-based work often does suffer from an absence of management control. The objectives are not clearly enough thought out, the target group is not clearly enough defined, the workers lack support and supervision. This is not as it should be, and it seems to have led to a surprising degree of antipathy to project-based work—a feeling in certain quarters that it is not what the Youth Service is for, that it is untried and that its apparently free and easy style is far too unaccountable. This seems most unfortunate, since the two modes of working—centre-based and project-based—seem to us complementary: a well-founded local strategy should include both, and not only in urban areas. As with other fields of Youth Service work, full-time and part-time workers, including volunteers, can appropriately be used. Obviously both centre-based and project-based modes need their own appropriate arrangements for management control and supervision, and links with other services such as Intermediate Treatment and social service provision; but these are perhaps especially important in the case of project-based work. It is sometimes said that it is difficult or even impossible to evaluate 'detached' work. It is of course difficult to evaluate youth work of any kind: the mere presence of young people in a club is no indication that anything purposeful is happening there. If problems have arisen in the management of project-based work, we think it is because inadequate thought has been given to proper planning and proper reporting and supervision procedures. It is in the nature of this work that the worker is in an isolated position, and it is esential that the management structure should take account of this. There has been no lack of reports and studies on the planning and management of detached work, and we hope that these will be more widely studied and acted upon.

Some Essential Aspects of Provision

Participation

5.17   As we noted in chapter 1, the participative style was recognised quite early to be necessary to meet young people's developmental needs. It is a simple fact of management that a service is apt to be more effective and efficient if there is satisfactory machinery for consulting and involving the beneficiaries, but the primary purpose of participation in the Youth Service is to give the young individual a sense of belonging, a sense of identity, and the skills, confidence and assurance needed to participate not only in his club or organisation but also in society at large. This is a large and important claim. What is the Youth Service doing about it in practice? This was one of the questions we invariably asked on our visits to different localities, and it is an area frequently mentioned in evidence we have received. The only answer seems to be that some success has been achieved, but it is patchy and uncertain. There are encouraging signs, but much more effort needs to be put in.

38

5.18 The meaning of the term varies according to the degree to which participation takes place within the organisation concerned. The four styles of running an organisation distinguished in an earlier chapter (3.28) define the broad range. The authoritarian style allows for no participation; the paternalistic style for some, but on an informal basis; limited participation may apply to certain defined contexts and activities; full participation takes place where young people are responsible for organising and running the unit or activity concerned. Modalities also differ: many formal models have been evolved and can be seen in operation in different organisations, ranging from token representation, through various forms of shared or parallel management, to a fully democratic structure.

5.19 Any assessment of the current situation must start with the particular context or setting for which provision is being made. There is, first, the level of the *activity group*—football team, disco, or some other activity to which some members are committed. Secondly, there is the level of the *club or organisation* itself—its policy, management and finances. Thirdly, there is the level of *local affairs*, including not only the local Youth Service, but also other matters of local interest such as education, care of the aged and the disabled, library service, extending to issues such as housing and racial discrimination. Fourthly, there is the level of the *national youth organisations* and the extent to which young people are involved in the overall direction of their policy. Fifthly, there is a whole range of *national and international* issues in which young people may be involved.

5.20 Broadly we have found that at the *first* of these levels (the activity group) there is a considerable measure of membership involvement. In some organisations activity groups are more or less self-programming. At the *second* level (the club or organisation) there is much less evidence of this. Some youth workers told us that there were real difficulties involved when it came to entrusting matters of management and finance to the decision of young people. We appreciate that there are problems in this area. We did, however, see other clubs where these difficulties had been overcome and the young people had a large measure of control in these matters. Some leaders said that they had tried giving young people power to take decisions and had discovered after a time that they were not interested, were involved for a time but lost interest, or did nothing but talk without producing anything constructive. Others said that, once a satisfactory structure had been set up, the young people participated actively. It seems clear that the style, skill and commitment of the individual worker are crucial factors.

5.21 The *third* level (local affairs) is largely represented by the local youth councils which have come into being in a number of areas. Where they exist they seem to be liked and respected, and the level of participation is generally high; but there are not many of them, and the quality is variable. Sometimes they present the appearance of a debating society, much enjoyed by those young people who are given to that sort of thing, and encouraged by local authorities (through the use of their council chambers and so on) who see their youth councils as 'safe' forms of political education. Elsewhere more serious, informed and thoroughgoing involvement in local affairs is in evidence. At the *fourth* level (national youth organisations) the extent of participation varies greatly from one national voluntary organisation to another. Some organisations, such as the National Federation of Young Farmers' Clubs, provide a model of genuine member participation at national level: others still have a long way to go. At the *fifth* level (national and international affairs) there is a great range of pressure groups which many young people are involved with, and there have been several campaigns launched by young people or youth organisations. There is also a representative youth forum, the British Youth Council, which lobbies the Government on issues of importance to young people. Its view is sometimes sought by different government departments and other agencies.

5.22   Our view on all this, in brief, is that participation should be strengthened at all levels but not through imposition of any standard pattern. By this we mean:

(1) Participation at one level should not necessitate participation at another. There is no need to engineer a progression from one level of responsibility to another, but rather to provide a wide range of participative opportunities. A significant number of young people who have no interest in running their own clubs may well be interested in local community interests and vice versa. There should be opportunties in a variety of contexts.

(2) At club or unit level, members should have a high degree of control over the programme and facilities. This does not necessarily mean the adoption of set forms of organisation which typify adult arrangements, though one reason for the importance of participation at this level is preparation for adult roles. A wide range of structures work in different circumstances. The approach which is indefensible is accepting apathy as a reason for doing nothing. Apathy is an understandable reaction by young people to the situation of being without power and influence. It is the duty of the Youth Service to offer a positive challenge to their view of themselves and their abilities and to explore many different ways of doing this.

(3) At the level of the local youth council, efficient structures are necessary to ensure wide representation and to enable a fairly large assembly to function at all. But some of the ceremonial trappings and the formal machinery of holding committee meetings could well be dispensed with, to make way for real and serious debate about things that matter. Youth councils should be involved in action as well as discussion, and need to be built into the local policy-making machinery. A useful report from the British Youth Council*, funded by a DES grant, has signposted a way for future development.

(4) At both club and youth council level it is essential that the decisions and proposals of young people should be followed up. If there are delays and difficulties, reasons should be given and information fed back. Likewise, before and later, full and accurate information should be supplied to the young people concerned.

---

*'A Democratic Voice? The Changing Role of Youth Councils' by John Denham and Martin Notley (BYC, 1982).

(5) A strong stimulus to local youth groups is provided by meetings with other similar groups from different parts of the country or region. Too often, groups attempt to develop participation in complete isolation from each other. In this situation a group can become too reliant on a particular worker, and if he or she should go performance is apt to tail off. National organisations can play a useful role in helping bring different groups together.

(6) All the above depend on youth workers having the appropriate commitment, style and skills to encourage participation. Training materials such as those produced by a DES-funded project at the National Council for Voluntary Youth Services* are helpful in developing appropriate attitudes. Youth workers must be careful not to allow their own interests and expectations to colour the young people's range of interests, and must expect that on occasions their own position will be vulnerable.

(7) To equip workers for this role, initial and in-service training programmes should place more emphasis on the whole subject of participation.

Information, Advice and Counselling

5.23   Many young people have difficulty in gaining information about what is expected of them in given situations, about what they should expect from others and about opportunities which are available. They have a strong desire to discuss, both with their peers and adults, a whole range of matters which may have associated problems. It is important that young people have access to someone they can easily approach, someone they feel they can trust to understand their point of view and who is also well informed. Young people also need to have access to people trained in counselling skills to offer personal support on those occasions when information and advice are not of themselves adequate.

5.24   It is clear from our survey that by far the greatest amount of advice and information is obtained by young people from their families or friends, including friends of their own age; but they need facilities for approaching others on occasions when they cannot or do not wish to use their normal sources. Usually these occasions will be critical ones, and there is the more reason that the extra facilities should be sound, trustworthy, personal and confidential.

5.25   A number of agencies exist to provide such information, advice and counselling—some connected with the Youth Service, some not. Television and radio programmes may provide a service by phone-in or response to letters, and magazines may give advice by letter. Various services offer advice by telephone. Specialist advice is available on particular problems or subjects from national organisations outside the Youth Service, but the significance of the type of provision associated with the Youth Service is that it addresses the more personal problems of young people, and may come into play at an earlier stage in the

---

*'Young People and Decisions: A Resource Pack on Participation' by Martin Shaw and Alison Foster (NCVYS, 1981).

41

development of those problems, before perhaps they have been specially identified. By the same token, youth workers must be ready to refer young people to more specialised agencies if a particular problem is identified.

5.26   There are broadly three ways in which the Youth Service strives to meet this need:

(1) In most clubs and centre-based organisations adult workers, whether full-time, part-time or voluntary, normally find themselves in information, advice and counselling work. It is obviously impossible to quantify how much goes on. The familiarity and ease of the surroundings which favour this method also make it impossible to measure. In such surroundings also young people may do much to help one another. This is clearly an important strand in clubs and centres, and it would be a strange job specification for a youth worker which did not take account of it.

(2) There is a heavy emphasis on information, advice and counselling in what we have above called project-based work. While detached workers may aim to encourage activities of many different kinds, a basic factor is nearly always the provision of information, advice and help with personal difficulties.

(3) Over the past 10–15 years especially, a number of centres have come into existence specialising in youth counselling on a drop-in basis, or by phone or letter. These may be funded by LEAs, by large voluntary organisations or by small local bodies, and may use full-time, part-time and voluntary workers. As we might expect, many of these centres report great difficulty in funding, owing to the withdrawal or uncertainty of financial support. At the same time most agencies report steadily increasing usage.

5.27   It would be unfortunate in our view if any of these facilities were to be taken as excluding the others. The balance between them may vary from area to area, but each one has virtues which the other two do not possess, and the provision of suitable information, advice and counselling seems to us so important that the three methods may be taken as complementary, and all part of the mainstream of youth provision.

5.28   The implications of this are, first, that an assured place should be given to information, advice and counselling within the local planning of youth provision. Too often we have found that haphazard initiatives, often very good in themselves, are thought to be sufficient to meet the need, and there is no attempt to work them into a comprehensive policy. Account should be taken of which age-group the provision is for, the type of provision envisaged, the numbers and kinds of staff required and the location where the service is to be given. It should be the aim of local and national management to ensure that the various organisations involved can work together in a co-ordinated and co-operative way. It should not be left to the young people to find their way amidst a plethora of different channels of advice and help. It will normally be necessary that the planning, policy-making and management framework should be interdisciplinary, in the sense that the Youth Service will need to collaborate with schools, colleges of further education, the careers service, DHSS and social service departments, probation service, family planning agencies and many more besides.

5.29   Above all it seems essential that the funding of these operations should be put on a more regular and systematic basis. It is often the case that different sections of the official counselling facilities in an area are financed by different services in almost total isolation from one another, while the independent information, advice and counselling agencies struggle on from year to year with uncertain and tenuous funds. Multiple funding is probably inevitable in the circumstances, but this is no reason why an adequate and comprehensive budget plan should not be drawn up by all the services acting together, and appropriate assistance given to the voluntary agencies.

Community Involvement

5.30   Though various forms of service to the community are long established in the Youth Service, renewed emphasis was given to it from the early 1960s, springing from a conscious need to broaden the area of contact between education and society. The demand for more opportunities for young people, combined with a growing appreciation of the educational implications of such experience, led to the growth of a number of both local and national organisations, such as the Community Service Volunteers (CSV). The Youth Service Development Council commissioned in 1965 a report on the need for 'Facilities for the Co-ordination of Community Services by Young People', and a national independent organisation, the Young Volunteer Force Foundation (later to become the Community Projects Foundation), was set up in 1967. By this time a pattern of "clearing-house" organisations was established. These seek or accept referrals for service from institutions, social service departments, and others; assess the type of service required and the sort of volunteer best suited for it; allocate the task; and keep a check on performance.

5.31   This type of "community service" developed rapidly in schools and in higher and further education as well as in the Youth Service and was encouraged by the DES. During the same period the concept of community service gained currency as an alternative to custodial treatment for young offenders. More recently, since the initiative given by the Youth Opportunities Programme, community service schemes for the young unemployed have become a major option within that programme, and seem likely to continue with the new Youth Training Scheme. In this way the idea of community service, used mainly to mean an organised pattern of activity in which young people perform tasks which are of benefit to other members of the community, has become very widespread; and special merits are claimed for it as a form of social education particularly appropriate to the time.

5.32   Before we can state our view on this, it seems necessary to clarify what we mean by community involvement and relate it more clearly to the primary purposes of social education. The basic motive in most young people who are drawn to this sort of activity is in most cases a simple desire to help other individuals whom they see as disadvantaged in some way. Given an understanding of the local community this can lead to an impulse to seek to

43

understand the causes of disadvantage and if possible remove or lessen them; and for some at least of the young people concerned service to others is a stepping stone to active participation in community affairs, through projects aimed to affect the whole community, or sections of it, rather than individuals. We believe that this is a not only natural but also highly desirable progression in the personal development of the young individual. Whether one calls the whole process "service" or "action" is immaterial: perhaps "community involvement" would be the best term. It is our strong conviction that the process is an essential part of the social and political education curriculum which the Youth Service has to offer, provided that:

(1) it is at all points subject to the free choices and decisions of the participants;

(2) appropriate training is provided;

(3) it is undertaken in a context which encourages reflection on the experience gained;

(4) it embraces the whole spectrum of action from simple benevolence to participatory action in the community;

(5) the fieldworkers involved in organising opportunities are careful not to impose their own viewpoints or objectives on the young people involved, who should play their part in the planning and management; and

(6) the workers themselves are properly trained.

5.33 We make these points with some emphasis because although the widespread promotion of "community service" is welcome in many different ways, some confusion has resulted. We wish to repeat that community involvement in its full form embracing both "service" and "action" seems to us part of the mainstream of youth provision. It seems to have become associated in the minds of many people with young people who are in trouble or at risk, or less capable than the average of finding and keeping a job. Some see it as a way of achieving discipline. It is, however, clear to us that any form of compulsion and coercion would defeat the primary purpose of the activity. There needs to be maximum freedom of choice and opportunity, and there will no doubt continue to be a place both for large-scale national organisations and for locally based agencies. Not all will be connected with the Youth Service, but at least in those which are we would expect to see the features outlined in points (1)–(6) above.

Political Education

5.34 Politics is the term we apply to the forces which give society the shape and direction it has—*i.e.* which tend to change it or keep it as it is. These forces are based on attitudes—of individuals and of groups—and spring from the activity resulting from those attitudes—*i.e.* from people acting on their convictions. That activity can take certain institutionalised forms, such as voting in an election, joining a political party, engaging in canvassing etc. This is what most people think political action is. But political action can take place in a number of institutions in the community—for example, in industry or the churches—and can take forms such as making representations, getting up petitions, and in general trying to change the aspect of an institution, community or society which

44

impinges on the participant in an unacceptable way. Just as there are social skills which enable one to feel at home in society, so there are political skills which enable one to change it or keep it as it is if someone else is trying to change it.

5.35 In a democratic society it is inevitable and desirable that there should be a diversity of ideas and opinions. Our political tradition depends on consensus being reached on various issues. While it is accepted that differences cannot always be resolved, an understanding of and a respect for the views of others lies at the very heart of civilised and organised society. This implies a certain level of political literacy. Yet amongst the adult population there is widespread political illiteracy and indeed a failure to understand what "politics" is. Political education then is necessary. Our opinion survey seems to suggest that most young people see themselves as uninterested in politics but paradoxically hold strong views about a variety of issues which might be called political. We believe that, if they had a better knowledge of the processes by which change can be effected and greater skill and confidence in using them to put their views into effect, they would be less likely to resort to more violent methods of expressing their views about society.

5.36 The amount of political education actually carried on within the Youth Service seems to be relatively small. One national youth organisation estimated that only some 5% of its local units included any element of it in their programmes. The majority of LEA responses painted a similar picture with comments like "we have to be wary of that". We believe that this is dangerous.

5.37 Political education is not the same thing as political studies or civics though it may include some elements of civics. Much of the political education in schools or even within the Youth Service has this passive character. It is not enough. What is required is experience of such a kind that the young people learn to claim their right to influence the society in which they live and to have a say in how it is run. It is active participation in some form of political activity, formal or informal, which really counts. We have not found that such participation is at all widespread, and we shall examine in a moment some reasons for this. We must first, however, deal with two possible objections to the argument we are now putting forward.

5.38 It is sometimes argued that it is sufficient to provide information to young people or to expose them to those who hold conflicting views in some kind of "forum" or discussion evenings. Such methods have their place of course but they belong to the knowledge-imparting kind of political education, which we have argued is not enough. Again it may be argued that if young people want to learn about political activity they can always join one of the youth organisations associated with political parties. It is clearly important for young people to have an awareness of the views of all political persuasions, including extreme groups, and to learn how to evaluate them; but this of itself would provide only an inadequate understanding of the range of political action and knowledge as we have defined it. Such political involvement can result in membership of a wide range of organisations in addition to political parties.

5.39 The Youth Service has the potential to fulfil a much needed and vital role not only as a forum for the theory of political education but also as a scene of political activity addressed to issues which are of concern to young people. Through the internal machinery of their youth clubs or centres, through the wider scope offered by various forms of youth council in the locality, through participation in local and national issues, the Service can offer young people a real opportunity to express their views in the relatively "safe" context appropriate to the inexperience of those taking part.

5.40   It is at this point that difficulties begin to appear. Within the machinery of the Youth Service itself, as we have noted in 5.17−5.22 above, the fully participative style is not easy to manage. In political terms there is a real conflict between "safety" and "reality". For political education to be effective, risks have to be taken with the decision-making machinery of the youth club or local youth council. But to the extent that it is effective, young people and their leaders will naturally be led to look beyond the confines of the Youth Service itself and take part in wider issues. This inescapably incurs the risk of controversy and conflict. Where there are contending groups in the adult world, involved in economic, environmental or community questions, the dangers for young people are obvious. There is a real problem here which those who advocate political education within the Youth Service must surely face.

5.41   There is obviously no ready-made solution to this dilemma, which has always been a part of the regular experience of people with pastoral responsibility in any walk of life. We can offer some reflections and suggestions which may be helpful to youth workers, their managers and their employers, recognising that if political education is not a "safe" thing, neither is democracy, and one will not flourish without the other.

(1)   There should be more national recognition of the essential place of political education and of its implications. As it is, too much lip-service is paid to the virtues of the democratic society, without enough attention being paid to the risks and hard work involved. Later in this report we will be arguing for the establishment of a national body which can grapple with important issues of a practical or management nature. Such a body could help to focus attention on the place of political education within the Youth Service.

(2)   There should be more local discussion. With regard to the specific dilemma noted above, some observers have argued that it should be possible for youth workers to negotiate some kind of "contract" with their managing bodies or authorities, which would, so to speak, find the limits of their freedom in involving young people in political activity and so create "space" for legitimate activity. We doubt whether a charter of this kind would in fact stand up to the test in a specific case—partly because it would be impossible to foresee all the relevant circumstances, and partly because pieces of paper are apt to be thrown on one side when it comes to a pinch. Discussion and intercommunication between workers and management—with the full involvement of young people —are essential.

(3)   Management committees and other structures devised to help the individual worker should play a more active part and not leave the problem to the conscience of the individual.

(4) More attention should be paid in training courses, both initial and in-service, to the complexities and difficulties of the problem and the responsibilities of all interests concerned.

5.42 The problem is an aspect of the professional responsibility of individual youth workers. The above suggestions if followed may help to ensure that individual workers are not left in an exposed and isolated position, but in the last analysis they themselves have to give a lead. Training, experience and the supporting apparatus of supervision and management can reinforce personal integrity, but not supplant it.

International Aspects

5.43 We have so far considered young people's participation in and interaction with the world purely on a local or national scale. Clearly it is today more difficult than ever to confine considerations in this way. Many more people of all ages have experience of other countries through visits and holidays, and awareness of social, political, cultural and sporting events on the international scale is disseminated through television and other media. We have spoken earlier (in 5.34) of issues of a political kind which create interest and concern among young people. These are often of an international nature. Clearly questions such as the relations between East and West or the First and Third World are of interest to the whole community. More specifically, with its membership of the European Community and the Commonwealth, the United Kingdom has formal political links with some other countries.

5.44 It is possible to identify four broad types of international contact. First, there is a long history of youth exchanges and visits. These have recently increased. Exchanges are arranged, for example, between professional, sporting, cultural, handicapped and religious groups usually with assistance from government funds. Secondly, there are the World or European Federations of the Voluntary Youth Organisations. These provide an opportunity for young people from broadly similar organisations to meet together and gain an understanding of each other's history and culture. Thirdly, there are existing opportunities for young people to spend short or medium-term periods in other countries assisting with community development. This is achieved through exchanges of specialist staff and work camps. Lastly, there are contacts, particularly between national youth councils, throughout Europe and the Commonwealth. These may have a political nature and be concerned to put pressure on organisations like the European Community, the Council of Europe or the United Nations. These contacts provide an opportunity to consider common problems and to attempt to find common solutions. They also allow a greater understanding to be achieved by young people of different countries.

5.45 The opportunities that these international contacts create are often inadequately fulfilled. Young people themselves may be insufficiently involved in the planning; the groups are often small and unrepresentative; when abroad they may fail to have proper contact with the culture or young people in the country visited; and on return there is often too little reflection on the experiences gained or feedback into the general programme of their group.

Another cause for concern is the limited range of countries to which visits are made or from which young people come to this country.

5.46   There are many international projects organised in England which enable young people to share in the experience of international contact and understanding. It is important that youth organisations should be aware of these, as one of the ways of ensuring awareness of the international dimension among youth workers and young people.

5.47   *Summary of recommendations*

(1) The Youth Service has the duty to help all young people who have need of it. (5.2)

(2) The Youth Service's task is to provide social education. It has developed specific methods of working, including the experiential curriculum, voluntaryism, a non-authoritative relationship between workers and young people, and encouraging young people to participate in decision-making. All these modes of operation should be brought into play. (5.5—5.6)

(3) LEAS and voluntary bodies, in partnership, should ensure a more equitable geographical spread of Youth Service provision. (5.12)

(4) Provision for the over-16s is an urgent requirement. (5.13)

(5) Participation by young people should be strengthened at all levels—in activity groups, clubs, local affairs, national youth organisations and at the national and international levels. It may follow a variety of patterns. (5.19—5.22)

(6) An assured place should be given to provision of information, advice and counselling within planning of local provision. The providing authorities should give thought to this, and ensure that funding is on a regular and systematic basis. (5.28—5.29)

(7) Community involvement should be available for all young people with maximum freedom of choice and opportunity. (5.33)

(8) The provision of political education should be a normal part of the Youth Service curriculum, pursued in such ways as to involve active participation. Ways to bring this about include more attention to political education in training courses and active consideration at a national and local level, especially involving management committees. (5.36—5.41)

(9) Youth workers should build awareness of the international context into their work. (5.46)

CHAPTER 6: CHALLENGE AND RESPONSE

The response of the Youth Service to key issues which affect society generally. Involvement with other services. The need to make better use of resources through management and co-operation.

Alienated young people—long tradition of involvement by the Youth Service; difficulties of liaison with other services; Intermediate Treatment, the police— what the Youth Service can properly and usefully do.

Employment and unemployment: action by the Youth Service in two ways—in its own right and through co-operation with the Manpower Services Commission.

Education: new influences and trends which bring schools and further education closer to the Youth Service. Need for more coherent planning while retaining the special identity of the Youth Service.

Special needs in the inner cities: difficulty of multiple funding. Special needs in rural areas: high cost of essential services.

Role of the Youth Service in countering racism, and the importance of relating youth provision to ethnic community needs.

Equal opportunities for girls: where the Youth Service is failing.

Provision for the handicapped: integration, types of provision, and employment opportunities.

6.1   In many areas of modern society where special stresses arise, the Youth Service has to be particularly sensitive to the needs of young people and to develop special forms of response. In this chapter we shall be dealing with some of these special contexts.

6.2   There are certain themes which tend to run through most of them: the stressful conditions are not confined to the young, the problems which arise have their origin in some general factor in society, and a number of public services are involved. All this means that the Youth Service has to be particularly aware of how these services are operating (and vice versa). If sometimes these services, in their concern for the whole age-group, appear to be providing an "alternative" Youth Service, with obvious waste of resources, it must be rated a failure in management. We believe that it is equally necessary for the Youth Service to retain its distinctive and independent role, and at the same time for working relationships to develop between the various services concerned. This must obviously be a two-way process if resources are to be efficiently deployed.

The challenge of alienation

6.3   We have referred in chapter 2 to some of the features of our society which tend to promote alienation in young people. While our opinion survey has served to confirm the view of those who urge that we should keep a sense of proportion and not regard youth in general as a time of alarming and continuing crisis, it is equally important to recognise that for a significant minority alienation may result from either the long-term circumstances in which they find themselves or crisis situations which may arise. Some manifestations of alienation by young people bring them into direct conflict with adult perceptions of agreed social behaviour, and agencies other than the Youth Service, such as Intermediate Treatment (IT) and the police, intervene. Young people often feel that such agencies operate on adults' behalf and not in their own interest. The Youth Service is not normally perceived in quite the same way by young people. It has a duty to relate to these young people, wherever they are and however few they are, to prevent so far as possible crisis situations from arising and to provide support and help whenever alienation occurs.

6.4   The Service has in fact worked in such situations for years, partly in its traditional modes and more recently in a variety of other ways, such as through counselling centres and detached work. Youth workers are familiar with the pressures on young people which have been described in chapter 2, and with concomitant problems of homelessness, drug addiction, and delinquency. It is important to emphasise this because a certain amount of dissatisfaction has been expressed to us concerning the Youth Service's response to the situation of young people who are under stress on in difficulties. It is our impression that in many cases the shortcomings are of a management character. Much brilliant and effective work has been carried out by gifted individuals, but the contribution by the Service as a whole has been hindered by four factors:

(1) uncertainty and irregularity of funding;

(2) shortage of personnel;

(3) confused policies, especially as regards the proper relationship between crisis and normal activities; and

(4) uneasy and ill-defined relationships with the other agencies and services mentioned above.

6.5   The Service's involvement, or lack of it, in Intermediate Treatment may be taken as an example. When IT was originally introduced in 1973 it was expected that much of the provision would be made by the Youth Service and other community agencies, through referrals from social workers. IT schemes were drawn up listing hundreds of youth clubs and other community agencies. This expectation never materialised, despite considerable efforts on both sides in some areas, and social workers now provide IT in the main themselves, largely through activity-based groups. This has raised questions concerning the "alternative Youth Service" run by social service departments.

6.6   We have not studied this problem as deeply as it deserves, but the reasons for it seem to relate to all four of the factors mentioned above. In particular we have encountered the feeling amongst many youth workers that it is an essential principle of the Youth Service that young people should be accepted for what they are, without any labels such as "delinquent" or "at risk", and that their participation must be completely voluntary. Most workers have stressed to us that they do in fact work with young people who are in trouble in various ways, but they appear to be put off by or even positively recoil from the labelling process which they see as inherent in IT work, and indeed in the rescue work of the Social Services generally.

6.7 In spite of this there is involvement in IT. There is informal liaison at practitioner level; youth workers sometimes co-lead IT groups; young people on IT are sometimes referred to Youth Service facilities; the Youth Service sometimes provides facilities and equipment. Over and above all that, it is often the Youth Service which picks up young people after they have been through a course of IT, and which then has to do its best to restore a normal relationship with society. There is therefore every reason to think that a working relationship between the Youth Service and the social services is possible, can be fruitful, and is urgently needed. It is the proper task of management to open the way for and facilitate proper liaison at practitioner level and indeed to overcome resistances at that level if there are any. Gross waste of resources must occur if management does not accept the responsibility of setting this objective and seeing that it is carried out.

6.8 Relations with the police are another area in which the Youth Service is necessarily involved from time to time, but where often no consistent policy of collaboration has been worked out. It is clear that for various reasons the relations between many young people and the police are difficult: this is a matter for grave concern. The causes no doubt lie in attitudes on both sides. The Youth Service has the opportunity, and the duty, to work towards an improvement in this relationship, in the direction of greater understanding, mutual respect and tolerance; but again it often seems hampered by an insufficiently clear concept of its role and method. It should be accepted that youth workers can act as friends and advocates for young people in dealings with the police: this is often particularly necessary in the absence of other representation by parents, friends or legal advisers. It would be helpful if guidelines were laid down to assist the youth worker in situations calling for this professional role; and training in their application should be included in initial and in-service course programmes. The Youth Service would then be in a position to make a contribution towards police training and to provide advice on police methods and practice as they affect young people. It is not enough for individual youth workers to work out their own relationship with police officers: a closer relationship is needed at management level between the Youth Service and the police.

6.9 To sum up, we consider it essential that the Youth Service, in following up its proper concern for the personal development of all young people, including those in difficulties, should develop appropriate relationships with those agencies and services which also have dealings with such young people. There is a clear need for interaction, each service observing its proper limits but co-operating to the fullest extent with the others. The Youth Service for its part is not concerned with "surveillance" or "control", but it can contribute to work with young people at risk or in trouble in the following ways:

(1) by providing places where such young people can become involved in activities in an informal atmosphere;

(2) by offering young people personal counselling and sometimes intervention on their behalf;

51

(3) by providing constructive relationships with adults and other young people;

(4) by offering alienated young people alternative ways of putting over their point of view and by enabling them to play an active part in altering their condition; and

(5) by representing young people's needs and interests to the other services and negotiating appropriate referral arrangements.

6.10 It seems to us important that all related services working with young people should enter into negotiations with one another on the basis of a schedule of aims and objectives such as the above. The three services mentioned in this section should in particular work together, by respecting one another's proper sphere of activity and principles, by contributing to one another's staff development, and by exploiting all possible opportunities for co-operative enterprises and transfer-funding.

The challenge of employment and unemployment

6.11 If we had been writing this report as recently as three or four years ago, one of the principal areas for discussion would undoubtedly have been how the Youth Service could play a part in "the transition from school to work". The plight of young people who remain unemployed after leaving school would have been a subsidiary theme, with the emphasis on improving their chances of finding work. The major theme would have no doubt been the relationship between the experience of work and a young person's personal development, and how this could be optimised, in terms of freedom of choice and the opportunity of training and further education.

6.12 Today the situation of being in transition from school to work often no longer applies. The submissions we have received from LEAs and voluntary bodies alike testify that a situtation is fast approaching, or is already upon us, in which the majority of young people leaving school at the minimum age may well have no prospect of a job. Against the background of increasing numbers of young people not occupied during the day by either full-time education or employment, the Youth Service has to consider what its role should be, both in providing facilities and activities for unemployed young people, and in sustaining their social confidence, skills and motivations.

6.13 It is this prospect which most preoccupies young people. Getting a job or not getting one will be found to be the most common topic of conversation in youth clubs. Unemployment and employment alike are events which the Service simply has to build into its curriculum of personal development. There are two aspects to this involvement. One is how to succour and support those young people who are at risk of having their personal development stultified by the experience of unemployment. The other aspect is rather different. Over the last year or two there has been progress towards the introduction of a comprehensive system of education and training for young people who leave full-time education. This aspect underlies the Youth Training Scheme proposed by the Manpower Service Commission (MSC) and now backed by the Government. It is clear that there is a great deal of work still to be done to realise the full promise of those proposals. What is to be the Youth Service's contribution to this work?

6.14 Let us begin with this latter aspect. At an early stage the Review Group expressed the view to the MSC that, if the prospectus towards which they were working was to be "foundation training for all young people whether employed or unemployed", then the scope of the enterprise was far wider than that covered by traditional training for long-term employment in particular (mostly skilled) occupations. For many, perhaps most, of those young people likely to come within the scheme it would probably represent their only link with any kind of structured pesonal development programme. A range of approaches and providers would be required, reflecting the diversity of the needs of the young people concerned. It would not be enough to provide just vocational skills training and work experience. If young people were to retain employability through periods of unemployment and be able to respond to unforeseen job requirements, then vocational training would have to be complemented by a corresponding personal and social development to provide the necessary maturity for employment and the confidence and coping skills needed to retain this employability. We are glad to note that these views are shared by the MSC and the Government. It is in this area that the Youth Service has in our view a crucial role to play.

6.15 Considerable experience has been gained over the last few years, partly by further education colleges working on Unified Vocational Preparation schemes, partly by the MSC itself through the Youth Opportunities Programme (YOP), but also through the work with unemployed young people carried out by Youth Service agencies. This has shown that successful vocational preparation depends as much on the "process" of learning as on the content. Student-centred and experiential learning and particularly participatory methods, aiming at motivation from perceived relevance, are widely recognised as desirable approaches for all young people, and certainly essential for the less qualified and motivated. While claiming no monopoly of these approaches, the Youth Service has always given them emphasis, and they have been the basis underlying the substantial successful work with the young unemployed pioneered by a number of LEAs, by the Young Men's Christian Associations in their 'Training for Life' programme, by the Community Industry scheme initiated by the National Association of Youth Clubs, and by the Community Service Volunteers' 'Springboard' scheme.

6.16 It seems to us therefore critically important that the Youth Service should participate fully in the planning, delivery and management of the new Youth Training Scheme. We shall be referring in 8.38−8.39 to the liaison structures necessary for this. Here we wish to characterise briefly the input which the Youth Service can make.

(1) *Staff training and development:* a variety of models of initial and in-service training are available, and the youth and community work training agencies themselves could be used. The question of "training the trainers" is one to which insufficient attention seems to have been given to date.

(2) *Curriculum development:* the examples already mentioned—and there are many others—show that the Youth Service has much to offer in

working out a curriculum which is both experiential and flexible enough to make individual needs.

(3) *Trained and experienced personnel:* many youth workers, both full-time and part-time, are already involved in work with the unemployed and, if the necessary financial support were forthcoming, this side of their work could be expanded relatively quickly. The expertise available would comprise life and social skills work, activities such as workshops, community projects and so on, and counselling on both an individual and group basis.

(4) *Residential and outdoor pursuits centres:* many LEAs and Youth Service agencies have such facilities, with the skilled staff to run them. They could be exploited as an essential resource both for personal development work and staff training.

(5) *Sponsorship:* both statutory and voluntary agencies in the Youth Service can and do play a major part as sponsors or managing agents of schemes, in particular community projects and training workshops.

(6) *Young people's views:* both in the planning and the management of the Youth Training Scheme (YTS), and in making its specific contribution to the delivery as outlined above, the Youth Service has the special function of speaking as an advocate for young people and helping representatives of the trainees themselves to make their views known.

6.17   The precise way in which these resources of expertise, staff and premises are brought into use for the YTS in any particular area will obviously be a matter for negotiation, and we shall return to this point later. It is clear that a cost will be involved, but, given appropriate planning, consultation and management procedures, it should be possible to optimise the use of existing resources. Some of these funds will come directly or indirectly from the MSC; but in our view it would jeopardise the success of the whole scheme if LEAs were prevented, through financial constraint, from playing their essential part in rationalising existing provision and developing new initiatives. Already there are many instances which we have seen where local education authorities have set up machinery, often based on their Youth and Community Service, to stimulate and co-ordinate the development of sponsored projects. We believe that voluntary youth organisations are likely to welcome a lead of this sort. This initiatory and co-ordinating function could embrace a number of aspects critical to the future development of the YTS, *e.g.*

(1) assisting and enabling sponsors, whether local authority departments, voluntary bodies or employers, to understand the criteria and prepare acceptable plans;

(2) advising on the personal development curriculum of projects put forward by sponsors, including outside employers;

(3) organising work experience within local authority departments; and

(4) helping to prepare suitable arrangements for training and supervising the trainers themselves.

6.18   It should not be supposed that Youth Service involvement with the young unemployed should be confined to the role of sponsor or enabler of MSC schemes, nor that of advocate for Youth Service methods in a MSC setting. As noted in 6.13 above, there remains for the Youth Service its own distinctive and necessary work in furthering the social education of all young people whether employed or unemployed, and whether on a YTS scheme or not. Provision of the kind offered by the Youth Service will continue to be needed for young people who are receiving YTS training, and even more for those for whom no suitable schemes are available or who remain unemployed after taking a YTS scheme. Account will need to be taken of regional geography, type of location, ethnic background, social grouping and sex. In general it seems inevitable that the Youth Service will need to develop new methods of countering the devastating consequences on individuals of both unemployment and also of dead-end employment. The fruits of much hard work and planning are already beginning to appear in some areas. Many youth clubs now open for periods in the day-time, and more will have to do so. More centres are needed, together with project-based work, to cope not just with the officially unemployed but also with the unseen unemployed—those who are too discouraged even to approach a Job Centre. Some developments are taking place in co-ordinated multi-agency provision, where a number of separate initiatives providing for different youth needs work together to provide a comprehensive service which may embrace, for example, housing, employment or basic education as well as social education. LEAs can help to ensure that the information data and skills of different services are brought together: it seems clear, for example, that practice in the Careers Service and in the Youth Service could be more closely aligned. All these developments will cost money on staffing and on premises, but a great deal can be achieved through proper deployment of existing resources.

The challenge of educational change

6.19   As we have seen in chapter 3, for all young people below 16 and a number over that age their experience in full-time or part-time education in schools and colleges of further education is an important factor. A smaller number of the age-group we are concerned with will be involved in higher education. The Youth Service will therefore need to take full account of changes in the educational sector.

6.20   Various pressures and influences have been acting on educational institutions, and thus the context today will be a different one from that in which earlier reports on the Youth Service were written. During the last twenty years, the move towards the creation of comprehensive schools and the greater, if scarcely universal, acceptance of pupil-centred methods of teaching and formal systems of pastoral care have all left their mark on the secondary school.

6.21   More recent influences are concerned with the school's relationship to and place in society. There is a general feeling that the curriculum is too important to be left solely to local and, to some extent, chance decisions, but must be scrutinised to ensure coherence, balance and relevance to the young person's future as well as present needs. It is felt that the community has a legitimate interest in what is taught in schools, and this has focused attention on curriculum matters. An effect of this has been more emphasis on social studies, courses for personal skills, and programmes to help young people prepare for citizenship and other aspects of adulthood. The move towards greater accountability has also created movements for more parental involvement in schools and more direct influence by governors and, in some cases, school councils. Financially difficult circumstances have also forced greater attention on "value for money" and the practical merit of courses.

6.22   Fewer young people will mean fewer teachers, so that teachers' average age and length of stay in post will increase, with perhaps both negative and positive effect on their morale and school life. The need for a more educated population and more especially perhaps the difficulty young people have in obtaining employment have led to a steadily increasing proportion staying on at school beyond the minimum leaving age (though the proportion remains lower than in some comparable countries). Young people now staying on are often those for whom the traditional academic offerings of sixth forms are not suitable, as they do not expect to continue into higher education.

6.23   The same range of influences is also affecting both full-time and part-time further education. Courses developed at the lower level of qualification for the Business Education Council and the Technician Education Council and by the City and Guilds of London Insititute (some of which are developing in schools also) contain large elements of training in personal skills; and the new courses which have been introduced in connection with the MSC provision and pre-vocational preparation involve a special emphasis on personal development.

6.24   Personal development has of course in the past been an important part of the implicit programmes of schools at least, but the particular form and urgency it now takes on with the new post-16 clientele are evoking new responses in the field of curriculum development. It may be sufficient to mention here as an example the proposals recently brought forward, after much public discussion, for a new qualification for such young people, provisionally known as the Certificate of Pre-Vocational Education, and designed to measure ability to make informed choices about employment, knowledgeability about different types of occupation and the relationship of these to society, and personal development generally. Statements about the purpose of the courses which would lead to this qualification tend to mention the development of personal attributes such as self-motivation, adaptability and the capacity to work constructively with others. The need for counselling as part of the course is also noted. It seems clear that the introduction of such concepts into the school curriculum will radically affect what the schools offer to all young people in the years preceding the statutory school-leaving age, as well as in the years following it.

6.25   It will already have been noted that the language in which these changes are described has a close affinity with the objectives of the Youth Service on the one hand and with those of the Youth Training Scheme for which the MSC is responsible on the other. The developments outlined above mean that groups of young people at school, in further education or on Youth Training Schemes may well be involved in provision which, while distinct, has large elements in common. In some areas this convergence of aims and methods as between the Youth Service and the schools has received explicit recognition through the joint appointment of an individual as both a youth worker and a member of a school staff. In some cases such individuals may find a field of operation in youth wings attached to schools. There are arguments both for and against such arrangements. It makes sense that youth workers should be involved in planning curricula and programmes in schools, and also that the facilities of schools should be open for use by the Youth Service: we have seen good examples of both. But we have also seen examples where the marriage has not worked: the youth wing is used by a limited number of school pupils in the day-time, but the evening work is quite separate, and there is little real contact between school use and community use. There are other ways also in which the two services can come together, *e.g.* through jointly planned periods of residential experience. Underlying all such formal arrangements, and running well beyond them, is a growing need for the Youth Service to contribute towards the shaping of school curricula and programmes, and vice versa.

6.26 It is to be hoped that LEAs will not see this convergence of aims and methods as an occasion for confusing the roles of the two services. They each have their part to play, and they play it most effectively not by keeping each other at arm's length but by negotiating on the basis of the values which each hold to be most important. A common language is an immense advantage in this respect, but does not imply that the independent status of each service should not be preserved. Here therefore is another case where management must accept responsibility for negotiating collaborative arrangements, including the sharing of staff and facilities. The result will be not only a more effective use of available resources but also a more rational presentation to young people and to the general public of what schools and the Youth Service both have to offer.

The challenge of special community needs

6.27 Every environment or locality will have its particular character and associated problems, and we have noted how one of the special strengths of the Youth Service is its ability to respond to these. There are certain areas where a combination of particular difficulties produces a special situation.

Inner cities

6.28 Many inner-city areas suffer problems caused by their history, especially in post-War years. Special renewal and development have created areas of new populations but neither the traditions nor the facilities to service social needs. In some cases large numbers of people, including young people, with language difficulties compound the situation. Towns may have been specially created to deal with needs of industries which have themselves since changed or moved away. People in such areas will naturally be the first to suffer the effects of high levels of unemployment: this may lead to further deterioration in commercially based facilities for leisure or even shopping. Nor should it be assumed that deprived urban areas necesarily have the advantages of easy access and good transport. For people living in areas originally situated at the edge of towns, problems of infrequent transport may be added to the general barrenness of the modern urban environment. Funds made available under Section 11 of the Local Government Act 1966 or the Urban Programme may be able to alleviate some problems, but they are not always taken up or used in the most coherent and constructive ways.

6.29   Whilst the wide variey of Youth Service provision is applicable in inner-city areas, as elsewhere, and indeed some organisations have a strong tradition of such work, there are specific responses of the Youth Service which are particularly relevant:

(1) the inclusion of work with young people within a community development response to the needs of a neighbourhood;

(2) the provision of project-based work; and

(3) the identification, training and support of leadership from within the local community.

All this emphasises the particular need in inner-city areas for co-ordinated management. Currently there is confusion due to the variety of provision and policy-making at both national and local level. Various resources are now devoted to inner-city areas without the appropriate co-ordination which would lead to their being spent most judiciously. This confusion leads to the isolation of the Youth Service and youth workers from other agencies with whom they should be co-operating closely.

Rural areas

6.30   The provision for young people in rural areas has its particular problems too, and these are exacerbated by too little recognition of this fact in either general or specific funding. The changing pattern of agriculture and its associated industries has led to rural depopulation, which has in turn resulted in loss of communal facilities. It is obviously more difficult to maintain the community life of the village, including that of its young people, if the traditional meeting places such as village schools, churches, shops and pubs have closed. Young people will move away, increasing the isolation of those left; and homes will be sold to retired people, or as second homes to owners who may well bring new life to a village but not for the younger age-group.

6.31   Young people are adversely affected by the lack of transport in rural areas. For they will be reliant on others or else have no means of reaching those places where sufficient numbers allow viable Youth Service provision to be made. The scarcity and high cost of transport may present special difficulties for unemployed young people in reaching places where they can seek work or undergo training.

6.32   The difficulties of achieving viable numbers result in higher unit-costs. Yet the weightings determining grant distribution and given for additional educational need bias the funds towards urban areas. Minimal weight is given to a factor of sparsity, which would benefit rural areas. In addition, these areas do not in general have access to specific grants such as those made under the Urban Programme or Section 11. This leads to the paradoxical situation that, though provision per capita is more costly in rural areas, less per capita is generally spent, causing a wide disparity of provision by comparison with urban areas.

6.33   Clearly it is difficult to provide a comprehensive Youth Service in all rural areas. It is important, however, when discussing and seeking solutions to problems of rural deprivation that the needs of young people are also considered. Obiviously they should be given the maximum possible use of community facilities, such as village halls, and there should be the maximum dual use of schools. In addition, the employment of a youth and community worker to work with a variety of age-groups or alternatively a joint teacher/youth worker appointment helps the provision of professional support to youth groups in rural areas. Where alternatives to traditional types of public transport, such as community buses, are started, attention should be given to the difficulties which children who are bussed to school experience in participating in after-school activities of any sort. Residential provision may be the most appropriate for certain activities.

6.34   The major difficulty that those in rural areas face is that their numbers are small, their difficulties go unnoticed and resources are not provided. Their forms of alienation may be as acute as those in urban areas and may be compunded by their isolation. The solution requires not only a fair share of resources but also appropriate styles of work, support and provision.

The challenge of a multi-cultural society

Countering racism

6.35   Young people from an ethnic and particularly black community encounter difficulties beyond the ordinary which are not of their making. These include the possibility of a clash of loyalties and interests springing from differences in cultural backgrounds and social norm. This factor is very variable: it affects certain groups of young people quite seriously (*e.g.* Asian girls), others hardly at all. Other difficulties obviously include reduced opportunities of employment, which impact more strongly in general on black youths than on white (though again there are differences in the way this factor affects different ethnic groups); and also rigidities in the educational system and deficiencies in housing. But there is one special factor which is part of the common experience of all ethnic groups in this country. This is the experience of racial discrimination and prejudice, whether it is exercised in open, concealed or largely unconscious ways. A service which is concerned with the personal development of young people must not fail to take this factor into account.

6.36   We are not concerned at this point so much with considering what specific kinds of provision the Youth Service can most appropriately make for young people from ethnic communities: we shall be dealing with that later. Here we wish rather to address ourselves to the *facts* of racism, *i.e.* to the undeniable existence on a wide scale, in all age-groups and most sectors of society, of an attitude of antipathy towards fellow citizens who have a different colour, a different ethnic origin, and possibly some different social and behavioural traits. This attitude is not universal, and it no doubt springs in the main from social and economic insecurities in those who harbour it, but it cannot be argued away and is an evil with potentially disastrous effects both on those who display it and those who suffer it. Can the Youth Service, with its concern for balanced personal development in all young people, do anything to counter racism?

6.37   It is obvious that the Youth Service is only one amongst a number of agencies which have a responsibility in this regard. Indeed, on its own, the Youth

Service is likely to achieve little if it finds itself at odds with the combined forces of home, officialdom, the education service, the employment sector, the media and the police. Racism is only likely to yield when all these forces are working together against it. But it is right that the Youth Service should ask itself what its specific contribution should be.

6.38   There are in our view three principal ways in which the Youth Service can make its influence felt: by making itself fully multi-cultural in its outlook and curriculum; by exploiting its capacity to lobby and campaign for equal opportunities and appropiate community development; and by introducing a measure of "positive action" into its management practices. These should be the objectives of the Service in areas where there is little cultural diversity just as much as in areas where there is a great deal.

6.39   First, then, the Service needs to embrace whole-heartedly the concept of cultural diversity as a positive gain in any society. This strand of thought is already present in many youth movements, but it has perhaps tended to manifest itself more in international relationships than in practical inter-cultural activities at home. Discussions, projects, community service and action can all play their parts as elements within a multi-cultural curriculum. Where separate provision for certain ethnic groups seems appropriate, it is all the more important that cultural bridges should be built. In particular the Youth Service may be one of the few agencies with the capability or the will to do something about those elements amongst *white* youth which are vulnerable to manipulation by racist organisations. All youth organisations should, and many do, commit themselves to building defences against such manipulation; and there is scope for greater efforts in various forms of outreach work through detached workers and advisory centres.

6.40   Secondly, as we have noted in chapter 5, the Youth Service has a public face in the community. Action within the community is one of its tools, used to further the social and political education of its members. It has an opportunity here to bring home to the public both the realities of racism and the ways in which it may be broken down. Young people themselves may be the best creators of a more equal and unprejudiced society.

6.41   Finally, the Youth Service should adopt management practices appropriate to these aims. This would mean, for example, fully involving black communities in the process of policy making and review, in curriculum development and in management structures, at all levels down to unit level; ensuring black representation at meetings and conferences; adopting recruitment policies which would ensure a conspicuous presence of black workers within the Service as a whole, *i.e.* not just in black areas, nor in the lower echelons of the Service; and most importantly insisting on a multi-cultural approach in all initial and in-service training courses, including racism awareness sessions for all white trainees, and in the arrangements for staff supervision.

6.42   There are no doubt resource implications here, which we shall consider in chapter 10, but much can be done within existing resources, given a firm commitment to the approaches outlined above.

6.43   In the literature of the Youth Service, provision for ethnic groups has tended to mean special provision for Asian and Afro-Caribbean communities, although in practice other communities have made distinguished contributions. This is because the former are numerous, unevenly distributed, increasingly of British birth, and black. They have tended to foster a sense of their own identity, though this is not usually felt to be specifically alien to that of British society in general, but rather something extra—a dual identity, one within in the other. Because of this and the nature of the community within which young people have grown up, because also their personal development will have been affected by the experience of racism and by the tendency of the media to thrust a "criminal image" upon them, the provision of social education for these young people may well have to take a specific form, both to enable the communities to preserve what they want to preserve and to assimilate what they want to assimilate, and to help the young people concerned to resist the disintegrating experiences to which they may have been subjected.

6.44   A true appreciation of this need has been slow to gather strength in this country. Some 15 years ago, the Hunt Report on 'Immigrants and the Youth Service' (1967) recommended that separate clubs for young people from ethnic communities should not be tolerated (except possibly in the case of Asian girls), and that provision should be made for all young people in an area, regardless of ethnic background, in integrated clubs. We now see that this is a naive approach. A Service which is dedicated to the principle of flexible response to the developmental needs of young people cannot be so wooden but must orient itself towards the values and needs of the communities from which the young people come. There is a good deal of evidence that ethnic groups look upon youth provision as closely linked with community development, and it can happen that they may actively distrust organisations which aim to give the young types of experience from which adults are excluded. This accounts for some of the specific observed differences between mono-racial black clubs and the white or mixed ones—the wider age-range, the "extended family" style of management, the way they tend to grow their own cadre of leaders, and the high level of attendance.

6.45   We repeat that the essential starting-point for youth provision must be the felt needs of the community. It should not necessarily be assumed the youth *club* as such is the best instrument for meeting an ethnic community's needs. Policy will need to be shaped with the fullest possible participation of the community itself. It may well be found that centres for sport, the arts, and other activities, without the constraints of formal membership and involving a relatively wide age-range, are preferred to club provision. It may be necessary to give a higher profile to the more experimental forms of provision, including project-based work in all its many varieties. But where club provision is desired, it should not necessarily be a matter of concern if the *de facto* membership at any particular time turns out to be all black or all white. It is more important to meet the needs of young people within their community than to aim at a theoretically integrationist policy. There is some evidence that, where a whole range of social policies is in force, covering housing, education, employment, police liaison and

61

so on, which are all working towards good community relations and the elimination of racism, mixed clubs in fact do well.

6.46   There is also some evidence to suggest that youth clubs closely associated with schools succeed in being mixed to a greater extent than other clubs and in including girls whose parents would not normally permit them to attend clubs. This is no doubt because the educational setting is thought to provide safe ground where community interests and values are not felt to be under threat. Too much should not be built on this. Youth wings have other advantages and seem a useful element in local provision in any case.

6.47   Where it seems likely that all-black or all-white clubs will be common, it will be for the Youth Service in an area to arrange for and support cultural cross-fertilization in other, unforced ways. Visits, arts festivals, inter-club activities all have their place. What we need is not just to accept but to welcome cultural diversity and to cultivate the outgoing attitude which has been typical of the best traditions of youth movement. The precise direction to be followed may only emerge after full and serious discussions with the community, which implies a full commitment by all those responsible for youth provision to the objectives outlined in paragraphs 6.39 and 6.41 above.

6.48   Provision along these lines, depending on the number and distribution of ethnic groups within a local population, may well mean a higher level of provision overall, especially so far as staffing is concerned. LEAs are well aware of this. The full-time and part-time staffing needs of a Youth and Community Service operating in such conditions call for urgent consideration of "positive action".

6.49   Youth work training has a particularly important part to play in ensuring that the correct approaches are adopted. There are two aspects to this. In the first place, the number of ethnic minority workers is still small in relation to the needs, and greater emphasis should be placed on recruiting and training suitable personnel. But it is not just a question of recruiting more ethnic minority people to courses of training. For all entrants, from whatever background they come, it is necessary that their training experience should stress the nature of the multi-racial society which this country has now become, and its implications for themselves and young people. In-service courses are also needed. We return to this point in chapter 9.

Creating equal opportunities for girls and women

6.50   It is impossible in undertaking any comprehensive study of the Youth Service not to become aware of a movement which is often described as "work with girls". This is a rather misleading title because it might give the impression that girls as such were a "problem" for the Youth Service. It seems to us that what we see here is rather an attempt to come to grips with a set of attitudes in society which affect the personal development of girls, to try to eradicate the deleterious effects of these attitudes from the Youth Service, and in so doing to give girls a better deal. Hence it seems appropriate to include this topic in our "Challenge and Response" chapter.

6.51 There have of course always been Youth Service organisations working largely or exclusively with girls and young women. These certainly address themselves specifically to the personal development of their members, and uniformed organisations such as the Girl Guides are popular and have increasing memberships. They do not appeal to all girls, however, and their main growth in membership is from the age-groups below 14. As regards the broad mass of young people aged 14 and over, the evidence suggests that, in terms of membership of youth groups of all kinds, the boys outnumber the girls by about 3:2; and that, in terms of their participation in activities and the use of facilities, the boys are much more conspicuous than this proportion would suggest. These facts alone should cause us to question whether the Youth Service is succeeding in its aim to enable every young person to fulfil his or her potential as an individual and as a member of society.

6.52 Attention has been focused on this issue in recent times by the general movement towards equal opportunities for women. Many sectors of society, including schooling, professional training and employment, are under scrutiny; and the Youth Service cannot escape this questioning. Indeed it must be particularly vulnerable to criticism if it is failing young women at the most impressionable period in their lives. The existence of the "work with girls" movement testifies to a growing concern that the Service is doing just that, not of course from set intent but because it uncritically mirrors sexist attitudes in society and has carried these into elements of its practice and philosophy. It is necessary that the Service should take deliberate steps to put this situation right.

6.53 Though we have mentioned girls' organisations and feel sure they will always have a place in the generality of youth work, we do not believe that mainstream provision should be segregated. It is not as though girls want to do different things from boys or need a different curriculum. They need rather to have equal participation in much the same range of activities. The long-term aim for the Youth Service, as for society in general, must be to ensure for girls the same range of opportunity and access as boys have; and this should take place for the most part in a mixed setting (though separate provision should always be an option). It may however be necessary, as workers with girls often urge, and always depending on the local factors of geography, socio-economic conditions and so on, to envisage for the time being an increase in separate provision for girls *within* the mixed setting of a club or organisation. This may be needed to build up and sustain social confidence, to prevent the exclusion and discouragement which may result from the dominance of activities by boys, and to provide space and time to develop new activities if these are desired. What we have in mind, therefore, is an increase in the setting aside of places and time within an organisation in which girls can meet together without boys for discussion or simply to enjoy activities on their own, *e.g.* through the provision of girls' nights, girls' outings or girls' week-ends. This may require an increase in the provision of material, such as tapes or slides, appropriate to such occasions, and in the allocation of more sessions so far as staffing is concerned. In order that this provision should be successful and a source of experiential learning for both boys and girls, and male and female workers, it is important that the justification for separate girls' provision and the implications for boys and men of challenging male and female stereotypes are studied and understood by workers and young people alike.

6.54 With regard to the long term, we envisage progress being made towards equality of opportunity in the following directions.

(1) *Curriculum:* The operating styles which we have noted in the Youth Service—participation, advice and counselling, community involvement and so on—all provide scope for a concerted effort to promote reflection on the status of girls and women and on the validity of current social attitudes. Ingrained attidues can be challenged and unconscious assumptions brought to the surface. In short, the Youth Service curriculum should be committeed to the eradication of sexist attitudes.

(2) *Project-based work:* While space can and should be made for these processes in the club setting, it is significant that much recent work with girls takes the form of detached work. This is a further reason for expanding this type of provision.

(3) *Training:* It has been mentioned several times in evidence to us that work with girls does not figure prominently in training programmes, whether initial or in-service, for full-time or for part-time workers. It is in training pre-eminently that the "hidden agenda" of assumptions and values can be questioned and tested. We therefore believe that courses and curricula need careful re-assessment, not in order to incorporate "work with girls" as a problem area of study, but with a view to promoting greater sensitivity to girls' needs in general.

(4) *Staffing and management:* One of the most important needs is to correct the present imbalance between men and women in the full-time worker and officer force. (See 9.4.) We do *not* mean that there should be more female workers available to work with girls. We mean rather that more women should be taking their place alongside men in work with both girls and boys. At officer level women are grossly under- represented, and we believe that this cannot fail to blunt the impact which the Youth Service should be making on sexist attitudes. At management level generally, in committees and consultative groups, the Service should be seen to be committed to equal status and opportunity.

(5) *Resources:* Many LEAs have seen a need for modest additional expenditure *e.g.* on staffing, training programmes, conferences expenses and information material. This seems to us necessary, though much can be done within existing resources, provided the right policies are adopted and suitable monitoring procedures introduced.

Work with the handicapped

6.55 Provision for handicapped young people has in a sense been part of the tradition of the Youth Service from its earliest days; but systematic provision having regard to the number of handicapped young people in an area, their location and their specific type of handicap has been a development largely of the last 10–15 years with the increasing emphasis on community provision. In this development both LEAs and voluntary bodies have played a notable part: the former in funding or grant-aiding the salaries of workers and organisers, providing premises and transport, and helping to organise training; the latter in raising funds, increasing public awareness and launching local initiatives, activities and organisations. The following paragraphs are written not so much in criticism of the efforts already being made as in an attempt to pinpoint areas of weakness which could be rectified if they were sufficiently widely recognised.

6.56 It has become commonplace, to quote the slogan of the International Year for Disabled People, to say that "disabled people are people". Integration within the community is the aim accepted by all authorities and governments. The apparent simplicity of this principle does not of course mean that the problems of implementation are simple ones. It is important to remember that disabilities are complex and diverse: there are impairments of the sensory and motor functions, impairments of the intellectual functions, and impairments of a psychiatric or behavioural kind; and they can arise in combinations. Handicap is created by situations—by the effect of the disability itself on the individual, but also by the environment in which that individual is operating and by the attitude of people around him or her. Integration is concerned with meeting for the handicapped basic needs felt by all people—relationships with an acceptance by the peer group, and participation in activities, groups and the community. The process may involve separate groupings for the handicapped at some stages but, as an ultimate aim, it requires as full a participation in normal activities and relationships as possible. Some youth bodies and clubs or units are organised to meet this aim. It seems to us that, in order to ensure integration in any meaningful sense, providing bodies in an area should resort to a variety of means, including both integrated and separate provision. Those who have given us the most thoughtful evidence stress above all the need for a conscious and well-informed policy for a particular area, based on firm data about the numbers of handicapped young people, their whereabouts, their type of disability and their contacts and background. Merely to secure such a data base is not easy. Another important consideration is that information about facilities and opportunities should constantly be made available to the handicapped themselves, who should have a full say in what is offered.

6.57 The types of provision which will flow from such a policy will need, as we have indicated, to be diverse. In principle one would expect to find the same elements as we have identified in youth provision generally, such as facilities for meeting and socialising, facilities for sport, travel, holiday visits, art, music, drama and so on. Informed observers stress the need for counselling and advice; and a noteworthy feature of much successful provision for young handicapped people is the extent to which it involves community action. This is a field in which the handicapped young person has as much to offer as the non-handicapped.

6.58 There are some constant needs which run through all this diversity. One is transport, which is often the key to putting ordinary living within reach of the handicapped. Voluntary efforts have achieved much and will no doubt continue to do so, but there will also be a need for increased public expenditure. There is also a constant need for relatively minor expenditure on the facilities of clubs, centres and other provision so that, for example, the physically handicapped are not debarred by the absence of a toilet which they can use or a ramp for a wheelchair. There is also need for constant review of provision made for specific

65

disabled groups in particular clubs or centres to see whether modification of general provision or activities, or preparation of "ordinary" young people can assist in overcoming difficulties of communication in the case of the sensorily impaired, or of reaction in the case of the mentally handicapped. They all have normal needs, and many can be met in normal situations if they can be given confidence and independence. A further constant need of overriding importance is the need for awareness training and preparation at every level—for the able-bodied club members, for youth workers, for officers and management, and for the local public. This will usually mean allocating a definite responsibility for these things to nominated officers.

6.59   Finally, there is a need specific to the field of the handicapped to provide opportunities of employment in which they can participate. We have seen what employment means to a young person and what efforts are being made to meet this need for those who are not handicapped. For the handicapped, who have the same need, special provision may be necessary. Though employers may be ready to co-operate in providing jobs for handicapped young people, continuing support and counselling may be necessary to ensure that disappointments do not occur. There are places where this need is being met, but the picture is patchy.

6.60   Thus again we see that there are organisational requirements which are not always and everywhere matched by appropriate policies or by co-ordinated effort. Resources may be wasted if policy is lacking or not being followed up.

6.61   *Summary of recommendations*

(1)   The Youth Service and other services dealing with young people should develop the means of working together. It is the responsibility of management to foster collaborative arrangements with other services, whilst respecting the independence and proper role of each. This will encourage the most effective use of funds, staff and facilities. (6.3−6.10)

(2)   The Youth Service has an esential role in helping to provide facilities and activities for unemployed young people; in sustaining their social confidence, skills and motivation; and in making a contribution, including the sponsorship of courses, to the planning, delivery and management of the Youth Training Scheme. Provision will be needed for those young people for whom no suitable training is available, who are still unemployed after training, or who find themselves in dead-end employment. (6.11−6.18)

(3)   Converging aims and methods make it all the more necessary that the Youth Service should contribute to the work and curriculum of schools and colleges. (6.19−6.26)

(4)   There is a special need for co-ordinated management in the inner cities. (6.27−6.29)

(5)   In rural areas, attention should be paid to providing equitable funding and appropriate styles of provision. (6.30−6.34)

(6)   The Youth Service in common with other agencies and services has a duty to combat racism in all its forms. (6.35−6.42)

(7) The needs of ethnic communities should be recognised in the planning, management and delivery of local youth provision. (6.43–6.49)

(8) The Service should take deliberate steps to ensure that the personal development of girls is not hindered by confused or reactionary attitudes to the role of women in society or by sexist attitudes in the Service itself. The personal development needs of girls in mixed settings may need to be catered for by an increase, for a time, in separate provision. (6.50–6.54)

(9) The integration of handicapped young people into the community implies a variety of provision, both integrated and separate. (6.55–6.60).

CHAPTER 7: CONCLUSION TO PART 2: A YOUTH SERVICE FOR THE 1980s

The main characteristics of the Youth Service in the future, in terms of objectives, offerings and age-ranges.

7.1 The conclusions reached in the earlier chapters of this part of our report enable us to pinpoint the elements of the future pattern of youth provision. In saying this we do not mean that we expect there to be a standard pattern. Local needs and priorities differ widely, and must be locally determined. But it seems to us equally necessary to identify the elements which should assume importance, in differing degrees in different areas, if the local provision is to be complete and adequate. Within this local pattern there is of course an unassailable place for the great national organisations which have served young people over the years; but these organisations are usually the first to acknowledge their local roots and their responsiveness to local needs. The relationship between all the forms of provision in an area is one of the issues we consider later: at this point we are simply characterising in a general way the facilities which should be made available by local authorities and voluntary bodies working together, for the provision, other than through full-time education or full-time employment, of social and political education for young people over a wide age-range.

Objectives

7.2 The Service has great achievements to its credit, but further advance is hindered by a lack of clearly stated objectives. There is no lack of discussion within the Service and outside it about what its aims should be: this is normal and right, and the professional associations within the Service play a notable part. From our study of this extensive debate we conclude that what the Service needs is not so much a set of entirely new objectives as a restatement of its existing ones. What is lacking is a public acknowledgement of and a general consensus about what the Service is trying to do.

7.3 We believe that a basis for this consensus undoubtedly exists. There is virtual unanimity that the fundamental purpose of the Youth Service is to provide programmes of personal development comprising, in shorthand terms, social and political education. The significance of these terms has been discussed in preceding chapters. We reiterate here that in our view there need not and should not be any antithesis between personal development and social education. The one is to be read in the light of the other. Social education does not mean social control any more than personal development means anarchy. The twin aims of this process are thus *affirmation* and *involvement*—affirming an individual in his or her proper identity and involving an individual in relationships with other individuals and institutions.

7.4 We repeat here that we see social education as essentially an experiential process, as opposed to the passive reception of ideas, impressions and norms. It involves experimentation—the trying out of modes of behaviour and styles of action in a way calculated to help young individuals to know themselves and be able to cope with (though not necessarily to accept all the implicit values of) the society of which they find themselves a part. From this premise it follows that the process of social education must above all be *participatory*. It is not enough to provide places to go to and things to do. The Youth Service must make it its business to create opportunities for young people to have a say in their affairs and to organise their own activities. This is one of the oldest themes in discussion and writing about the Youth Service: its effective realisation remains one of the keenest challenges for the future.

7.5   It follows also that what we have described as *political education* has an essential place within the Youth Service's curriculm. Just as social education is not the same thing as social studies (or moral education the same as ethics), so political education goes beyond the study of political systems or civics, though it may include something of the latter. Basically it must mean the process whereby a young individual learns how to claim the right of a member of a democratic society to influence that society and to have a say in how it affects him or her. This requires practice as well as study. Like all social education, political education is an active, participative process.

7.6   A further aspect which we should not overlook is what we may loosely call *spiritual development*. There is a sense in which the reality of this, though not perhaps the term, is always close to the minds of many youth workers and indeed most young people. In some groups or organisations it may take a very specific or doctrinal form: in others such forms are eschewed, but the underlying values are strongly emphasised. What is in point here is the need, explicitly or implicitly recognised, to acknowledge aspects of the human condition which are not purely practical and prudential. There are two propositions which are basic.

(1)   It is necessary for the process of human development that the individual should preserve a sense of wonder and gratitude for life and what it brings: this sense lies at the root of enjoyment, interest and appreciation, and without it an individual may well be thought to be maimed in some essential way.

(2)   It is equally essential that human relationships should be based on an absolute respect for other human beings, and indeed for other living things.

In our increasingly multi-cultural, multi-religious, multi-ethnic society it must be part of the Youth Service's function to uphold both propositions in all it says and does, and to enable young people to formulate and develop their own beliefs.

Offerings

7.7   The Youth Service has many different things to offer young people and it must continue to offer this variety, mixed in various ways and proportions to suit the needs of different communities and age-ranges. The proportions in which these offerings are mixed can only be a matter for local decision, with the

69

full participation of the young people themselves; but it may be useful here to summarise the main elements as the five "A"s:

association,

activities,

advice,

action,

access.

7.8 *Association*

By this we mean, as Albemarle meant, a place to go, a place to meet, a place to be with friends, a place of refuge other than the home, a place for socialising and enjoyment. There is no doubt that this is one of the features of the Youth Service by which young people themselves set store. It is one of its most widely recognised features, not only in clubs but in other forms of provision also; and what we have said in 7.4 above should not be taken to mean that we underrate it. It is a basic foundation.

7.9 *Activities*

These again in all their increasingly rich variety are a vital as well as a traditional feature of youth provision. They may not be ends in themselves, but they are a basic element. The Youth Service must offer young people interesting things to do, new things to test their prowess and adaptability, opportunities of fresh experience, things to exercise the body and mind. For all the increasing range of youth activities, the variety is probably not sufficient in most areas. The range should include popular sports and pastimes, but not be confined to them. The arts should have an important role. The provision of an appropriately wide range of activities is a challenge to the ingenuity and administrative expertise of providing bodies.

7.10 *Advice*

We use this term in a wide sense to denote the whole process of providing information, advice and personal counselling. Young people need all these, and receive much, through home, school, the churches, official services such as the careers service, and various specialised agencies. This is not a reason for the Youth Service to opt out. It may equally be a first resort or a last resort—somewhere to go when you don't know where to get advice, or somewhere to go when other sources fail. Important questions will arise over how information, advice and counselling should be provided in any particular area. Of the three methods described earlier (in 5.26)—provision within a club, provision as part of detached or project work, and specialised local agencies—none seems sufficient in itself. In order to provide an adequate coverage a mixture of all three will usually be necessary, and it will be essential to build up liaison arrangements with related counselling services run by, for example, the social services and the Careers Service. There is therefore much to be done to put the pattern of provision in this field on a satisfactory footing. It must henceforth take its place as one of the mainstream forms of youth provision.

7.11 Action in the Community

This embraces the various forms of community service which are part of the established tradition of the youth movement, but our term runs wider and has a different starting point. The concept of service presupposes a sense of obligation to the established order of society which may be a product of personal development but cannot be taken for granted. The concept of action has many roots—in some, simple compassion for other individuals, in others a desire to acquire an identity as part of a larger community, in others again a wish to remove the causes of distress by changing aspects of the environment or the society. Whatever activites are built upon this basis, it is essential that they should be freely chosen by the young themselves, should be undertaken in a context which encourages reflection on the experience gained, and should encourage a wider and deeper involvement in community affairs. To introduce any form of coercion or compulsion can only defeat the primary purpose of this activity. We envisage community action taking place within the Youth Service in many shapes and forms. Much occasional activity falls within the scope of clubs and units of the uniformed organisations. At local level many young people are involved in youth councils which are active in the local communities. Regular part-time experience can be provided through locally based and financed organisations, a number of which have come into existence over the past 10 to 15 years. Substantial periods of full-time service are most often associated with large-scale national organisation. To make this diversified array meaningful and known to the general public and especially to young people is an administrative challenge which we think the Youth Service must face. It seems likely that the key to future development will lie with local agencies, sometimes statutory, sometimes voluntary, acting in collaboration with other organisations including schools.

7.12 Access to Life and Vocational Skills

By virtue of its personal style of approach, the Youth Service seems to us to have a vital role to play in all initiatives designed to mediate the transition from full-time education to adult life. Within the broad spectrum of education and training opportunities, it will not be sufficient to concentrate on full-time study on the one hand and skill training and work experience on the other. Education and training must be complemented by personal development to provide the confidence and coping skills which young people need, whether to find a job and keep it or to retain their balance and initiative through periods of unsettling technological and economic change. This is an area where the Manpower Services Commission and other sponsoring agencies need help from the Youth Service: conversely, it seems essential that the Youth Service should look on access to vocational and life skills as part of its mainstream provision, as it already does in certain areas. The extension and development of this work will be a difficult process; but we think that the Youth Service should take the long view and play its part in an overdue step towards a comprehensive system of vocational training and experience for the employed and unemployed alike. At the same time the Service has its own specific part to play in building up confidence in those young people who are especially disadvantaged by unemployment.

71

7.13 All the five modes of operation described above can take place in a project-based setting as well as in clubs, centres and uniformed units; and it seems clear that they should do so. The precise manner in which the five modes are worked out to produce a comprehensive youth policy in any particular area must be a matter for local evaluation and decision, though we believe that there is a place for national stimulation, supervision and monitoring. The machinery needed for this purpose at local and national level will be the theme of the next chapter.

Age-ranges

7.14 It is at first sight surprising that the question of age-range figures so largely in discussion about the Youth Service, since nowhere are any statutory age-limits laid down. Circular 1486 set 14 as the lower age-limit, that being the statutory school-leaving age of the time. But Circular 13 of November 1944 explicitly extended the age-range downwards to cover those still in full-time education; and there has never been any basis for an upper age-limit, other than the age of national service, when this still applied. Although the present Education Acts are silent on the matter, the consensus has been that the age-range was 14-20.

7.15 It is no doubt a convenience for providing bodies to have some target-group in mind, but different local authorities and voluntary bodies have approached the matter in different ways. In theory all would probably agree that the determining factors should be the sociological and psychological boundaries which mark the beginning and end of the shift from the dependency of childhood to the independence of adulthood. This is not a very workable definition. Some would put the beginning of the end of dependency as early as 7 or 8, and a number of voluntary organisations and LEAs have junior divisions which start at that age. The age of 11-12 is seen by many as a significant turning point, and the statutory school-leaving age, now 16, as another. The upper age-limit has generally been equated vaguely with the likelihood of marriage and the assumption of increased responsibilities in the early 20s.

7.16 At its widest, therefore, the age-range with which the Youth Service has to deal may be conceived as extending from about 7 to about 25, and it is for consideration whether this broad range needs stricter definition or some kind of prioritising. We believe that there is a valid field of social education running right through this wide age-range, and that there is no point in trying to be too precise about the extreme boundaries. It has to be remembered that few activities or forms of provision span the whole age-range. Most are normally confined to, or chiefly manifested in, certain strata. Social education will naturally take different forms at different ages. The point which exercises most people is whether priority should be accorded to any particular stratum, and whether this priority should be reflected in statutory duties, as distinct from statutory powers.

7.17 Varying views will be found concerning the priority to be attached to one or other of four broad bands, viz: 7–10 years, 11–14 years, 15–19 years and 20–25 years. From the evidence available to us it appears that the great majority of LEAs and voluntary bodies concur in thinking that the 11–14 and 15–19 age-groups should have priority over the two outer bands. The 15–19 age-group is widely seen as that where the severest stresses are encountered and where the need for support is greatest. Recent events such as the onset of unemployment have reinforced this view. On the other hand, many believe that in order to withstand these stresses the defences must be laid down in the 11–14 band, while certain youth organisations attach great importance to the work that they do with the 7–10 age-group and have found this to be the most buoyant recruitment area in recent times. Some critics allege that the youth movement generally has tended to focus its attention on younger and younger age-groups because of a failure to meet the needs of the older ones. This is an inaccurate and simplistic view. Each age-group needs its own specific and different type of provision. The view shared by most voluntary organisations and LEAs, however, is that the 11–19 age-group should have priority.

7.18   We agree with this diagnosis; but we feel that the urgent concern which the Youth Service has for the unemployed extends to a particular role with young people who may have completed a scheme such as the Youth Training Scheme but still have not found employment. For this reason we believe that the priority age-range stated in the previous paragraph should be extended by two years at the upper limit. We believe that LEAs should continue to have a power to provide, or assist others to provide, for the whole age-group without specification of any boundaries. But, so far as statutory duties are concerned (with which we deal in chapter 11), it seems to us reasonable to define the age-range for this purpose as broadly extending from the 11th to the 21st birthday. We do not see this as an onerous requirement since the bulk of provision for this age-group is already on offer through a variety of agencies inside and outside the local authority. The Youth Service, as at present, will not need to make the whole of this provision, but we do envisage its role being enhanced.

7.19   *Summary of recommendations*

   (1) The overall aims of the Youth Service should be seen as affirming an individual's self-belief and encouraging participation in society. (7.3–7.5)

   (2) The Youth Service needs to acknowledge the need for the spiritual development of the individual. (7.6)

   (3) The mainstream offerings of the Youth Service by which it will achieve these aims are *association* (a place to meet); *activites; advice,* information and counselling; means to *action* in the community; and *access* to vocational and life skills. (7.7–7.13)

   (4) Local education authorities should continue to have the power to provide, or to assist other services to provide, for the whole age-group of young people. Statutory duties should embrace the ages 11–20. (7.14–7.18)

73

PART 3—STRUCTURES AND RESOURCES

CHAPTER 8: STRUCTURES

Need for improvement in administration of the Youth Service; functions of management. The national level: ministerial responsibility; arrangements for consultation and supervision—proposal for an advisory council; arrangements for information collection and policy support—role and management structure of National Youth Bureau. The local level: collaborative arrangements; liaison between local authority services; partnership between LEAs and voluntary bodies; representation of young people; liaison with the Youth Training Scheme through the Manpower Services Commission.

8.1 There are different kinds of creativity. The kind that matters most is that which takes place in the field, in the relationship between workers and young people, in the discovery of new ways to meet new needs, in the creation of trust and hope. But there is another sort of creativity which consists in facilitating and enabling these things to happen, proclaiming a common purpose and objective, and seeing that resources are matched to needs. This is what good and creative management is about. We have indicated at a number of points in this report that in general the Youth Service could be better managed. By this we do not mean that it is badly administered, but that, in certain ways crucial to its functioning, the concepts and philosophies by which management should work are often not clearly enough defined, and, partly as a result of this, the supporting structures which should aid that management are lacking or inappropriately referenced.

8.2 There is no real mystery about good management. It has four basic aspects—defining objectives, assigning roles, allocating resources and monitoring performance. These four activities change in nature and scope according to the level at which management is carried out, and therefore take one form at national level and another at local level. Where an appropriate structure, combined with the will and the skill to make it work, exists, the Service will function efficiently; but, where any of these is lacking, it will not. We are in no doubt about the good work of individual officers and workers: in this chapter we shall be examining the need for appropriate machinery to aid them in performing the four functions of management we have noted above, first at national level and then at local level.

The National Level

8.3 We have referred in earlier chapters to the confusion and uncertainty of purpose which results from the absence of a clear definition of the objectives of the Youth Service. This points to a failure at national level to perform one of the basic functions of management, and in our view it should be made good as a matter of urgency. There are three steps which should be taken as soon as possible. The first is to make better legislative provision for the Youth Service, defining its purposes and clarifying the responsibilities for it. This is such an important aspect of national management that we prefer to devote a whole chapter to it (chapter 11) and therefore defer for the moment the question of statutory provision. In this chapter we deal with the other two necessary steps—the clarification of ministerial responsibility and the setting up of appropriate administrative structures.

Ministerial Responsibility

8.4   We suggest that a Minister in the Department of Education and Science should be nominated to have responsibilities for co-ordinating the relevant aspects of the DES and other departments. The Minister should have a specific brief to negotiate on behalf of youth affairs at government level.

8.5   A number of other proposals have been put to us about ministerial and departmental responsibility, but we feel for various reasons that they would be likely to be less effective. Running through them all is a recognition of the problem that the Youth Service, as we use the term, constitutes only one of the many ways in which publicly recognised bodies intervene in the lives of young people. It is flanked by a number of other services, and we see no way of unifying all these under one management structure. Youth, as such, is no more a unitary and coherent field of public administration than old age or middle age would be. The concept of a Ministry of Youth, which would have to take over some responsibilities from the Department of Health and Social Security, others from the DES, and yet others from the Home Office and other departments, does not have much credibility.

8.6   There is, however, a much stronger case for some co-ordinating agency which, without attempting to wrest whole areas of responsibility away from other departments, would have the function of ensuring that those other departments carried out their responsibilities vis-à-vis young people in a co-ordinated way, and that resources were used as efficiently as possible. This is the gist of most of the proposals which have addressed the problem in recent years, and which refer in one way or another to a Minister who would have charge of this co-ordinating function. This is the concept we favour, but it needs working out with some care.

8.7   We do not attach credence to the idea of a co-ordinating Minister based in a separate department. Such a department would by hypothesis be a small one and, if its only function were to try to influence the youth policies of much larger and more powerful departments, the Minister would have to wage constant war along all its boundaries with no effective weapons. It is for this reason we have recommended nomination of a Minister in an existing department.

8.8   There are strong reasons why we feel that this Minister should be situated in the DES. Other departments are concerned with vital aspects of the lives of young people, but only the DES is concerned with the personal development of young people as such, and already has substantial servicing responsibilities in the youth field. We believe that this aspect must be the basic one; and, if the legislative proposals which we describe in chapter 11 are adopted, the DES, together with the education apparatus of local education authorities to which it relates, will carry certain statutory responsibilities which will make it appropriate, in our view, for the DES to carry also the co-ordinating role vis-à-vis other departments which have responsibilities towards young people.

8.9　It might perhaps be argued that the principle of Cabinet responsibility should relieve us of the need to carry our argument any further, since all Ministers consult their colleagues and the acts of Government are supposed to be one and indivisible. The problem is, however, a practical one: how to put a Minister based in one department in the best position to influence other departments, and have an overview of all aspects of Government policy which affect young people, *i.e.* the wide field of "youth affairs". It does not seem to us sufficient to leave such an important issue to the machinery of ministerial committees. The process of policy-making in the world of youth affairs, which requires regular and systematic consultation and exchange of information amongst many varied interests, requires machinery which is, and is manifestly seen to be, open and impartial. While final decisions are, of course, the responsibility of Ministers, the debate and deployment of fact and argument which will be carried on before decisions are made must be open to the public at large, and particular interests must have an opportunity to make up their minds and have their say.

8.10　These considerations make it essential in our view that there should be some national body charged with responsibility for advising Ministers on the exercise of their functions, in so far as these touch on youth affairs. There are various possible models for such a body, *e.g.*:

(1) an advisory council supported by an administrative unit which could be part of one of the departments with responsibilities in the youth field;

(2) a statutory commission plus an executive named and defined in an Act of Parliament; or

(3) a quasi-autonomous non-governmental organisation with a corporate identity conferred by a charter or deed, supported by grant and employing its own staff.

Of these, our preference would lie with the first, given the body's purpose and function. Its purposes would be to provide a focus for policy-making and for certain of the management functions which need to be carried out at national level, in particular those of framing objectives and monitoring performance. It would need to have a public face and a public address. But its function would be essentially to study, consult, and advise, not to act: it would be an advisory body that could conduct open debate and frame policies for transmission to the Government, but not implement them.

8.11　To the concept of an advisory council, however, we add two specific conditions. The first is that the body should be small and that its members should not be nominated representatives of any sectional interests in the youth field with which they might be connected. The problem here is a familiar one. Free and open communication and consultation would be required with all parts of the complex world of youth affairs. A forum is needed on which all parties can rely for impartial deliberation and judgement, and whose members will be of sufficient stature to ensure that its views carry due weight. The temptation is to set up a representative body giving a voice as of right to the various interests in play. Such a body would inevitably be large, and we do not believe that in this particular instance it would function effectively. The more realistic solution would be to appoint a fairly small number of individuals, including young people, in a personal capacity, chosen broadly for the varied experience they can bring to their task and the respect and weight which they would carry with the field and other interested groups. The best number would seem to lie somewhere between 15 and 20. Care would need to be taken that the membership was balanced, and there could be informal consultation with major interests in the field; but there should be no rights of nomination. Experience suggests that such a body does not need to be statutory or chartered, but its terms of reference should be clearly spelt out. We make some suggestions to this end in the annex attached to this chapter.

8.12   The other condition is more simply stated. It is that the council must be serviced by a unit which is publicly identifiable, and which does not appear to the public to be merely a part of a government department. The unit should have its own name and address, but there is no reason why the staff concerned should not be on the strength of a government department: this should clearly be the DES.

Arrangements for Information Collection and Policy Support

8.13   It is clear that an advisory council such as that recommended above would need to be able to draw upon accurate sources of information when deliberating and making recommendations. The collection and analysis of information is in fact part of the functions of a body which already exists; and we recommend that this body should continue, but with some modification and clarification. We refer here to the National Youth Bureau, which was set up as an independent charitable organisation in 1973 and is supported by a general administrative grant from the DES and by a number of specific grants for particular activities from certain other departments. Its functions are described in the Bureau's own words as "to act as a national resource centre for information, publication, training, research and development, and as a forum for association, discussion and joint action, for those involved in youth affairs and the social education of young people". Broadly speaking, therefore, the Bureau offers services to the field, as a clearing house for the collection and dissemination of information, as a support agency for groups in the field who are aiming to develop new ideas or techniques, and as an advocate of the Youth Service in general.

8.14   It seems clear that some of these functions, but not all, would be affected by setting up a new advisory body. We would expect the new body to act as a national forum for the development of new policy-thinking. There are, however, two essential activities which could be carried out better by a professionally oriented body having close links with field workers and voluntary organisations. These are the collection and analysis of data for the purpose of policy-making, and the spreading of information about good practice and new initiatives.

8.15   We have ourselves experienced difficulty over the first of these activities. (See 10.1). The difficulty largely arises from the dual nature of the Youth Service and the prominent role played by voluntary bodies and by volunteers. Accurate information about resources in this situation is hard to come by, and policy-makers are apt to find themselves making bricks without straw. The Bureau, as an independent organisation itself, should be able to make a real contribution here. The new advisory council might be expected to become an additional—and important—customer of the Bureau.

8.16   As regards the other activity, the essential problem is that of selectivity. We see a rough analogy here between the work we would like to see the Bureau doing and the work of a research council. The work would not be research so much as development, but the same criteria of "timeliness and promise" seem applicable. What seems to be needed is a flexible response to new initiatives in the field, coupled with a readiness to leave the running to others once a new initiative has established itself.

8.17   If these are accepted as the primary functions of the Bureau, there would appear to be two implications for its internal management. First, the Bureau should have an efficient selection mechanism for identifying new developments and rapidly marshalling the relevant information; secondly, its resources, particularly of staff, must be kept as manoeuverable as possible so that teams of workers on particular projects can be set up and stood down relatively quickly. It is not part of our business to try to evaluate the administrative efficiency of the Bureau but it seems appropriate to consider whether its structure is suited to the tasks it should be undertaking. It seems doubtful to us whether the present organisation of the Bureau passes the two criteria mentioned above.

8.18   There does not appear to be within the present structure any organ with the professional sensitivity required to meet the first criterion; and the composition of the council, and the role and function of the executive, should be carefully scrutinised with this point in mind. We believe that the purpose we envisage would be best served by a small appointed executive, with the freedom to consult the field as it thought appropriate, rather than by the current wide-ranging council, representative of youth affairs in general, with an elected executive, and a number of unit advisory committees.

8.19   As for the second criterion, it seems doubtful whether the present unit structure is really advantageous. While there is no objection to multiple funding from different departments as such—indeed, in view of the working of the Bureau, it is inevitable—it seems an error for this to be tied to specific units. It is all too easy for a unit to become self-perpetuating even though the original task for which it was set up and funded has been completed. In the present method of financing the Bureau, about half of the total budget of around £700,000 is met from a general grant-in-aid from the DES, while the rest comes from other departments and goes towards the support of the specialised units. Even though a cross-unit approach to certain topics is theoretically possible, inflexibility of resourcing is built in. The DES should remain the source of grant-in-aid, but we suggest that the Bureau's relationships with departments other than the DES could be re-negotiated in such a way that these departments "commission" certain kinds of enquiries or support work without actually funding units. The same "customer-contractor" relationship defined in a commission could also prove useful with certain areas in the field. In this way, the staff of the Bureau would not be placed in individual units and could easily transfer to other work once a particular commission was completed.

The Local Level

8.20 At the local level the same four management functions (see 8.2 above) need to be performed, but the problems associated with them take a different form. While the national level is concerned with general policy-making and review, the local level is concerned with the planning and delivery of specific services and activities. Emerging ideas and practices in the field need to be quickly assessed with a view to wider application; the proper role of all the different agencies needs to be established; and the available resources have to be directed to where they may be used to best advantage. This implies a continuous process of choice between one geographical area and another, between one agency and another, between one operating style and another. It is also essential that the performance of the local system should be continuously monitored. All this calls for collaboration between many different local interests.

8.21 The local authority in an area is in the best position to provide the focus for these management operations. We would go further and state that the role that we here envisage is particularly suitable for local *education* authorities, even though not all statutory services for youth come under education authorities. This is because the bulk of public physical resources available for young people lie within the control of local education departments and less tangible resources of experience, philosophy and policy-thinking also lie there. As we have stated earlier, the service of youth is fundamentally an education service, dedicated to the personal development of individuals, and by and large it is in education departments of local authorities that this sort of policy-thinking goes on.

8.22 This integrating role is far from easy, since it has so many dimensions, *e.g.*:

(1) between all the various services provided by a single authority;

(2) between the different tiers of local authorities;

(3) within the Youth Service, between so-called statutory provision made by the LEA itself and the services and facilities provi led by voluntary bodies;

(4) between the local authority services as a whole and the whole range of outside interests (many of which impinge on the lives of young people), including the media, commercial leisure-time provision, employment and training agencies, the machinery of law and order, and others.

Each of these dimensions calls for effective arrangements for ensuring communication and consultation in the formation of policy, and co-ordination in its execution.

Liaison between the Services of Single Local Authorities

8.23 It is a matter of frequent comment that there appears to be very little liaison between the various services of an individual authority. This gap may occur even between services operated by the same department, *e.g.* between schools and the Youth Service. Where this happens it is quite simply a matter of weak and ineffective management, and it is no good setting up specific structures to cure that. But where the liaison failure occurs between two separate departments of an authority, coming under two separate committees, it seems reasonable to look for structural faults. It is possible to find instances where, for example, youth workers and social workers have dealings with one another in their daily work and yet their respective managers and managing committees do not.

8.24   The concept of "corporate management" is the current local government response to criticism of this nature, but if it is interpreted as creating an abstract managerial function over and above the areas where the knowledge and competence of the individual sections to be managed lie, it will be a hindrance. What is essential is corporate planning embodied in appropriate structures. This can provide an officer framework. When elected members are required to answer for service provision, some authorities have found it convenient to set up an across-the-board committee to deal with boundary problems between departments. Another way is to give one powerful existing department an across-the-board remit in a particular area such as youth affairs. The problem of course is for that department to know sufficient of what goes on in other departments without a degree of detailed intervention which would be quite unworkable. Here lies the challenge to the concept of "corporate management".

8.25   Our own view, as we have said, is that the integrating function should be given to the education department, so far as the official structure is concerned. It seems right, however, that the public forum where substantial issues are discussed and exposed to public view should be the council of the authority.

8.26   There are two pitfalls which have to be avoided. One is that of nominalism, *i.e.* a tendency to adopt policies which appear to be integrationist but which are in fact vague and woolly. There is a danger of this happening in the case of the Youth Service through the widespread adoption of the concept of "youth and community development" or "community education". While the case for this style of approach can easily be seen, and indeed we have ourselves argued it, it is to be feared that the mere bracketing together of cognate services sheds no light on the policies and priorities appropriate to each, and may actually serve to conceal them. Where the structural form is broad, it is the more important that the policies governing each part of the structure should be clearly spelt out with due regard to the specific objectives of that part. Another danger which has to be avoided is the sort of arrogant professionalism which leads to professionals taking the attitude that they know best and belittling community response. This may happen when integrationist policies are being attempted because the response mechanisms developed within each particular service may be weakened when the services are brought together. The trouble is that the "community" is not one but many. In acting as the public forum, the council will need to ensure that all the cross-currents of public feeling are taken into account.

Liaison between Different Tiers of Local Authorities

8.27   This is a complex subject, and we are not qualified to deal with it to any extent. The point to be noted is that not all local authorities are education authorities, and some services, such as housing, are undertaken by authorities other than the local education authority for an area. To ensure co-ordinated planning and provision, therefore, a LEA will need to negotiate effective working relationships with different tiers of local government. We do not pretend to know how this can best be done; but there are areas where it is done, and the efficient delivery of services and use of resources demand that it be done. It is particularly necessary so far as the Youth Service is concerned because, as we have seen, it should have close links with services such as housing, social services and recreation which spread across more than one tier of local government.

Partnership within the Youth Service

8.28 The Youth Service is neither the property of local education authorities nor that of local youth organisations but the product of the two working together with each other and with young people. The management functions referred to above will therefore need to be jointly performed, and an effective management structure is needed for this.

8.29 There is no reason to think that this will be always and everywhere the same. There is room for a variety of local styles. Most local authorities have machinery for it, but its effectiveness varies greatly. There seem to be two main reasons for this. In the first instance the fault may lie in the terms of reference. It is necessary that these should clearly provide for the four management functions described in 8.2. This does not necessarily mean that the authority should be required always to act with the agreement of the voluntary interests: such a requirement would seem to offend against the political legitimacy and accountability of local government. Nor does it imply the compromising of a voluntary body's independence. It means that the authority should be required to communicate and consult, and that this communication and consultation should be, and manifestly be seen to be, regular and thorough, starting at a point where the voluntary bodies are able to make a genuine input into policy-thinking and not at a point where the policies begin to react on them. Some individual authorities at present have a pattern of customary links with the voluntary organisations which are active in their areas. This can and often does result in coherent strategies which reflect the level of involvement in policy-formation in those areas, but it does not happen in all authorities. Even where there are well-established procedures, these may be by-passed and the voluntary interests rendered powerless; and locally accepted priorities may conflict with regional ones, both in the local authority and the voluntary sectors. So there must be both machinery and the will to work it. Local authority members may well have their own particular allegiances to and links with individual voluntary services, but this cannot provide the necessary comprehensive input. We believe, therefore, that there should be, over and above the customary contact between statutory and voluntary services, a statutory obligation to create machinery of some kind to ensure regular and effective communication and consultation with voluntary organisations, over the whole field of the four management functions. We shall be including recommendations to this end in chapter 11.

8.30 The second main reason for poor liaison is that the voluntary sector is not always geared up to play its part collectively. The local authority side is fully equipped both for policy-making and for the delivery of services. If the voluntary sector remains simply a discrete collection of individual bodies each going their own way, vying with one another for the largest share of the available

81

resources, and with no capability for forming collective views or for reviewing their own performance, it will not be surprising if the local authorities call all the tunes.

8.31   We do not believe that the precise type of machinery required for all areas can be prescribed centrally. In some areas there is already effective partnership between statutory and voluntary agencies through a system of mixed committee structures which are truly representative of both sides. Where this works well, we would not wish to suggest a change. An alternative solution, which we think may be worth thinking about because it meets some of the difficulty noted in 8.30, is for the voluntary youth organisations to enter actively into appropriate independent *local consortia*, such as the present Councils for Voluntary Youth Services. Such bodies should include both local branches of national organisation and independent groups. Without interfering with the individual freedom of any one organisation, they could provide the voice which is best able to raise the view or views of the voluntary sector with its statutory partner. It is important that voluntary organisations give the right emphasis to the functions of these bodies. There is a danger that even with such machinery in existence they may fail to agree about policy objectives and concentrate simply on bidding for resources. Where this happens local authorities have no choice but to decide policy and priorities, and the Youth Service as a whole is likely to suffer. Without a strong expression of co-ordinated policy-thinking by the voluntary organisations, it is difficult to ensure that the resource implications of the Service are fairly and effectively weighed in discussions about budget allocations in local authorities. So the consortium must have appropriate machinery and use it to identify issues which need consideration, to engage in policy-thinking and review, and to accredit and brief their representatives on the authority's committees. The consortium will need to be linked in with the authority's committee structure.

8.32   In order to function effectively, a consortium will need administrative and staff support. As at present, this might be provided through the youth officers of particular voluntary bodies, or through their committee members. It may well be necessary to consider a specific appointment (paid or voluntary, full-time or part-time) not connected to any particular voluntary body. This administrative function should not be automatically seen as the province of the authority's own staff. Whilst a local authority may wish to support a consortium in its area, financially and in other ways, the servicing and administrative function should only be undertaken by an officer of the authority if this is the express wish of the consortium.

8.33   We have observed that, where the consortium approach is most effective, this is very often due to the institution of a small informal "preparatory group", consisting of some of the chief officers on both sides. The purpose of such a group is to keep the business of the consortium and the authority's committees in step, to plan the agenda and to follow up decisions. Its meetings should be regular but as informal as possible.

8.34   The foregoing paragraphs may have given the impression that the process described is a dialogue between two main interests, but in fact there is always a third—the young people themselves, though they do not always have an effective voice. We have spoken in chapter 5 about the importance of participation from the standpoint of social and political education. We believe that it is no less necessary from the point of view of effective management, and the local network must provide for it. There are various ways in which this can be done. To the extent that member participation is effective within both the statutory and voluntary organisations, young people will be helping to determine policy, and young people may well be involved through their organisations in the consortia or in management and advisory committees on the LEA side. But we also attach importance to the place within the local communication and consultative network of a *local youth council*, with a firm representative base in, for example, the local youth clubs, centres, uniformed organisations, schools and colleges. The main function of such a council would be to give coherence to the views of young people and to counter any tendency towards "tokenism" which might result if young people were only represented through particular youth organisations.

8.35   Whatever the fine detail may be, we would expect to see at the centre of the structure a *joint committee* serviced by the authority on which, in broadly equal numbers, representatives of the voluntary organisations (accredited and briefed by a local consortium or by some other means), representatives of young people (including those elected by the local youth council and from statutory youth provision in the area), and members and officers of the local authority take part in policy formulation, review and monitoring. Responsibility should be delegated to this committee for the deployment of financial resources in specific ways and within specific limits, subject to the overall policy and budget approved by the local authority. Meetings should take place at times and places convenient for young people.

8.36   As we have implied above, no structure is proof against malfunction if the will to make it work is lacking. It is essential that committed and influential people should be involved on both the LEA and the voluntary sides. We would expect all LEAs to follow the example of many in co-opting on to their statutory committees a broad cross-section of representatives of the joint committee described in 8.35 above.

Relationships between Local Authority Services and Outside Interests

8.37   Providing a focus for youth affairs in an area must mean effective communication and consultation with a whole host of interests over and above those of the local education authority and the voluntary youth organisations. The range of issues is potentially so wide that in general liaison functions have to be organised separately and ad hoc. It is, however, within the capacity of the local authority to provide a consultative forum and an official capability.

Collaboration with the Manpower Services Commission

8.38   We have already referred (in 6.16) to the part which we think the Youth Service should play in bringing to fruition the Government's plans for a comprehensive Youth Training Scheme (YTS). In its White Paper 'A Programme for Action' (Cmnd. 8455), the Government asked the Manpower

Services Commission (MSC) to organise the delivery of the scheme in such a way as to secure full local involvement, including that of local education authorities and voluntary bodies. Since then the Youth Task Group Report, published by the MSC in April 1982, has made recommendations about the local machinery required to secure the involvement and commitment of all the parties. We understand that these recommendations have been accepted, and would therefore expect that from April 1983 there will be some 50–60 local boards with boundaries related to LEA boundaries. They will have the key role of assessing the requirements in an area, establishing and supervising a network of managing agencies, mobilising support, and monitoring progress. We have from the outset made strong representations to the MSC that Youth Service organisations and personnel should be actively involved in local arrangements for planning and delivery of the YTS; and we were therefore glad to note the Task Group's recommendation that youth organisations should be represented along with others on the local boards. We believe that young people should also be represented. We are therefore now concerned to note that the arrangements proposed in the MSC's consultative paper on the future of local advisory machinery (May 1982) afford no place for the effective involvement of youth organisations and young people in the planning and delivery of the YTS. This would seriously weaken the scheme. If they are not directly represented, it is essential that their contribution should be secured in other ways.

8.39 While the Youth Service has an important part to play on the local supervisory boards, youth organisations, both statutory and voluntary, have an equally important and more pervasive place in the network of managing agencies and approved sponsors, as we have already indicated in chapter 6. It remains to make this input effective through full participation in the various management levels of the YTS.

8.40 *Summary of recommendations*

(1) The four basic management functions of setting objectives, assigning roles, allocating resources, and monitoring performance require appropriate structures for their fulfilment at national and local level. (8.2)

(2) The function of setting objectives for the Youth Service at national level could appropriately be fulfilled by means of legislation. (8.3)

(3) A Minister should be designated, based in the DES, to co-ordinate the work of all departments which have an interest in youth affairs. (8.4)

(4) An advisory council should be appointed to advise Ministers on youth affairs. It should consist of a small number of individuals appointed in a personal and non-representative capacity, broadly reflecting a wide range of youth interests. It should be serviced by the DES but have a distinct public identity. (8.10)

(5) The terms of reference and organisational structure of the National Youth Bureau should be reviewed to enable it to carry out more effectively the tasks of collecting and analysing data about youth affairs and of spreading information about good practice and innovation. (8.17–8.19)

(6) At local level the local education authority should be recognised as the prime focus for youth affairs and should be given a statutory responsibility for co-ordination in respect of the services of the local authority itself, as between different tiers of local government, and as between local authority services and the voluntary sector. (8.21–8.22)

(7) LEAs should be given a statutory duty to create machinery to ensure regular and effective communication and consultation with voluntary youth organisations, over the whole field of the four management functions. The precise form of this machinery should not be prescribed: scope should be left for local variation. (8.29–8.31)

(8) Voluntary youth organisations in an area should take steps to ensure that they have the capability of acting collectively in identifying and working out policy issues and playing their part in a partnership with the LEA. Local consortia, such as the present Councils for Voluntary Youth Services, may be appropriate for this purpose. (8.31)

(9) In order to function effectively, such a consortium will need administrative and staff support, which may well involve a specific appointment. It should not be assumed that this function will be undertaken by an officer of the LEA. (8.32)

(10) We attach importance to the role of local youth councils and to the effective involvement of young people in local decision-making structures. (8.34)

(11) At the centre of the local structure there should be a joint committee to which specific functions and powers should be delegated by the local authority. On it, representatives of voluntary organisations, of young people and of the local authority should work together to frame and review policy and to monitor performance. (8.35)

(12) Youth Service organisations and personnel should be actively involved in local arrangements for the planning and delivery of the proposed Youth Training Scheme, both as members of local boards and as managing agencies and sponsors. (8.38–8.39)

ANNEX TO CHAPTER 8

Proposal for an Advisory Council on Youth Affairs

1 The terms of reference of the Council would be:

(a) to advise the Secretary of State [for Education and Science, or other Secretaries of State as appropriate] on matters relating to the implications of Government policy for the personal development and welfare of young people in England;

(b) to keep under review the facilities provided in England for young people and to assess the effectiveness of that provision;

(c) to consider matters relating to the future development, resourcing and provision of the aforesaid facilities for young people;

(d) to prepare reports and other publications in order to bring the matters within its remit effectively to the attention of the public.

"Facilities provided for young people", as mentioned in (b) and (c) above, include facilities provided for the personal development and welfare of young people by whatever organisation outside the formal curriculum of schools and colleges, encompassing clubs for young people or with young people in membership or including provision for young people, projects working with young people, or other organisations involving young people. Providers may be central government, local authorities (both education authorities and others), voluntary organisations (both national and local), young people themselves and others.

2 Under these terms of reference the Council should expect to have referred to it for comment and advice all major new proposals affecting young people within the responsibilities of the Secretaries of State concerned. It should also be able to initiate studies and reviews of policy, practice and resources, both in the short and the long term, and refer its views to Ministers.

3 The Council would consist of not more than twenty persons appointed part-time for a fixed term in an individual capacity by the Secretary of State for Education and Science, after consultation with the Secretaries of State for Employment, the Environment, Health and Social Security, and Home Affairs. The range of interest and experience from which members would be drawn would include local authorities, voluntary organisations associated with young people, young people themselves, associations of professional and specialist staff for provision concerned with young people, and association of employers and trade unions. The composition of the Council should strike an appropriate balance between different age-groups, ethnic groups, and men and women. Assessors to the council would be nominated by the major administrative departments concerned, viz. Education and Science, Employment/MSC, Environment, Health and Social Security, and the Home Office.

4 The Chairman would be an independent person appointed part-time by the Secretary of State for Education and Science, subject to the same consultations as for members.

5 The Council would be serviced by a publicly identifiable administrative unit staff from the DES to be called the [Office of Youth Affairs].

CHAPTER 9:   STAFFING AND TRAINING

The tasks undertaken by adults in the Youth Service: face-to-face work and management. The general pattern of Youth Service staffing: the unique mixture of full-time, part-time and volunteer staff; the representation of women and ethnic minorities. Status of the profession. Full-time workers and officers: career considerations. The role of part-time staff. The crucial contribution of volunteers.

Training for youth work: survey of present arrangements, and of the critical issues raised in evidence. Need for a national supervisory body to assess and monitor both initial and in-service training; brief consideration of some of the issues which such a body should examine and review. Training for part-timers and volunteers: need to monitor and moderate local systems.

9.1   In the course of our enquiry we have met many of the men and women who work in the Youth Service—the youth workers, full-time and part-time, the officers, and the volunteer workers. We wish to pay tribute at the outset to the energy, enthusiasm and commitment which they bring to their varied roles, often in the face of much discouragement. In fact one of the first points to note about the work of the Youth Service is that it is both various and demanding. As the foregoing chapters will have made clear, the tasks which adults perform in the Service cover a wide spectrum, including both face-to-face work and management work as follows:

Face-to-face work

(1)   work directly with young people in providing social education, *i.e.* assisting them with their personal development through counsel and encouragement, organising activities and helping the young to organise their own activities, providing a supportive presence, and so on;

(2)   development work with communities, helping both young people and adults in the neighbourhood to identify their needs and to create for themselves the means of meeting these needs;

Management work

(3)   work with other adult staff, full-timers, part-timers and volunteers, in varying capacities including being colleagues in a team, participating in collaborative activities, leading and directing, supervising and training, and so on;

(4)   administration and finance, whether concerned with youth work in general in an area, or with a particular centre or project, including the preparation and processing of plans and budgets, consultation with management and other committees, the care and maintenance of premises, and all the paper work and telephoning that these processes inevitably involve.

These are only the main divisions: there are many variants and specialisms, but in one way or another these four types of work find their place in most job descriptions in the Youth Service. We turn now to consider, first, the various types of staff, their roles, numbers and career prospects; and, secondly, how they are trained and qualified.

The staffing of the Youth Service

9.2   Although fully trained professional staff play a critically important part in both the statutory and voluntary sectors, the Youth Service has what seems to be a unique characteristic amongst the caring services in the extensive use which is made of part-time and volunteer staff, and indeed in the facility with which people move from the volunteer to the part-time and to the full-time mode. The same sort of people may variously be part-time paid staff, or unpaid volunteers, according to local circumstances, and many of the full-time professional staff have begun their career in that way, achieving their qualifications through a course of initial or in-service training. Though the statistics are confusing and difficult to interpret in detail (see 10.11 – 10.13), a rough estimate of the pattern is as follows:

Employed by:	Full-time officers	Full-time workers	Part-time workers†	Unpaid volunteers
Local authorities*	900	2,400	15,000	100,000
Voluntary bodies	600	1,100	16,500	400,000 workers 23,000 officers

* a number of those employed by authorities work in the voluntary sector
† full-time equivalents

9.3   It should not be assumed that this remarkable ratio between full-time, part-time and volunteer workers is always and everywhere the same. It varies from one area to another according to local tradition and the policies currently being pursued, and it varies according to the types of youth provision. Thus in certain types of work, such as drop-in centres and project work, full-timers often predominate, though part-timers and volunteers can play a useful part. Counselling work, especially in the small local and independent centres, tends to involve full-timers, part-timers and volunteers in varying ratios. In clubs, whether run by LEAs or voluntary bodies, a full-time leader may be supported by a team of anything up to a score of part-timers and volunteers, some playing a general role and some bringing in special skills. Some clubs and units of the uniformed organisations are wholly staffed by volunteers. There are few public services where such staffing arrangements have even been attempted, and it must be counted to the credit of the Youth Service that it has developed methods of utilising this varied and flexible force of men and women, all highly motivated and committed to helping young people, and of instilling in them a professional approach.

9.4   The ratio between men and women in this force is also variable. For part-timers and volunteers, the Service has always depended heavily on married women. In the ranks of the full-time workers, however, the balance swings the other way—the men predominate by a factor of about 3:1 at officer level, men outnumber women even more strongly, by about 10:1. The proportions of men and women under training are more nearly equal, but it looks as if it will be some time before a more even balance works its way into the Service generally. Though there are understandable social reasons for this situation, which is not confined

88

to the Youth Service, it is a serious anomaly in a Service which is so largely concerned with the personal problems of both boys and girls.

9.5   A number of bodies have made the point to us that the proportion of full-time youth workers drawn from the ethnic minorities is small and that special steps should be taken to increase their numbers. We have referred in chapter 6 to the special needs of the ethnic communities and agree with this general criticism. It should be noted here that, so far as we have seen, the training agencies do give a measure of priority to entrants from ethnic minorities. Entry standards are reasonably flexible, and the number of students from ethnic minorities in training seems to be a higher proportion of the total number of students than the number of young people from ethnic minorities is of the total number of young people. These are imprecise observations, but they in no way invalidate the main point, which is simply that the Service as a whole and not just the ethnic communities would benefit if more workers came from the latter. The composition of the work-force would improve if in general more weight were given to previous experience and if more preliminary courses of study were provided. There is also growing concern that the recruitment and training of part-time youth workers from ethnic minorities and their access to full-time posts are insufficient.

9.6   There is one overall impression which we have derived from what we have seen and heard of this varied and impressive force. The men and women involved bring to their work many diverse skills, and yet we have encountered a feeling, especially perhaps amongst full-time workers, of being undervalued, of not being accorded a professional status commensurate with the responsibilities they carry or with that of their fellow workers in other services with whom they come into contact. This is a serious matter. The feeling seems to spring in part from their view that the Service in which they work is itself under-regarded and in particular does not have a satisfactory statutory basis. We make recommendations on this score in chapter 11. But there are other causes also. The routes to qualification are not as clear as many would like them to be, and the career structure is uncertain. As we observed in chapter 8, the Service also seems to lack good management: in other words, its objectives are not well enough defined, either nationally or at local level; roles are often not clearly enough assigned; resources are uncertain; and the apparatus of monitoring and assessment is sometimes completely absent. In particular, supervision in the sense of professional support, which must be considered essential in a profession which makes as total a demand on human resources as this one does, has not been developed to anything like the extent necessary.

Full-time workers and officers

9.7   *The full-time workers* in the Youth Service form a professional cadre: though they are relatively few in number, the Service could not exist in its present form without them. Their span of responsibility is wide, since all four types of work noted at the beginning of this chapter mingle and interact in the job specifications of nearly all full-time youth workers. In some cases we have found that this gives rise to confusion and even resentment. There is a feeling that centre or project administration takes excessive toll of the time of staff who are specifically trained to work with people; and also that work with young people has too often to yield place to work with other adults—organising, persuading, supporting, instructing, and so on. One of the problems is of course that the Service itself is undergoing rapid change, with the result that people often do not find themselves doing the precise jobs they were recruited to do. We have to state, however, that there is no way in which the full-time worker can escape from the fourfold responsibility outlined above—a point which must henceforth be kept firmly in the centre of all planning and curriculum development for initial and in-service training.

9.8   The composition of the full-time youth worker force is as varied as their roles. Just over a quarter will have entered the profession through an initial course of training in youth work (but often after part-time or volunteer experience). A few have social work qualifications. A substantial number are unqualified youth workers. But the largest category, about half, possess teaching qualifications and may or may not have had specialist training for youth work. We deal later (in 9.34) with the important question of whether a teaching qualification should without further training lead to full professional status within the Service.

9.9   If the routes into the profession are varied, those out of it are no less so. While a substantial cadre remains in the Service for life, the proportions of entrants (about 15−20% a year during the 1970s) and leavers (about 10−15%) are high, partly because there is mobility between youth work and a substantial number of allied occupations. Up to a point such mobility is both inevitable and desirable, given the relatively small full-time strength of the Service. It would be a problem for management to organise satisfactory career development if the Service were totally self-contained. But the amount of movement may well give rise to feelings of insecurity unless management takes the factor into account and does more to facilitate transfers in and out with due regard for relevant experience.

9.10   The turnover in full-time workers also poses the question of whether the grading structure of posts in the Youth Service provides sufficient incentive for good people to remain in it. We have in mind not so much the flexibility or suitability of salary grades as the accepted definition of posts. The criticism is sometimes made that the progression from youth worker to posts of higher responsibility is too shallow and abrupt. In order to further their career, it is said, youth workers must enter the ranks of middle management and become youth officers, thereby cutting themselves off from the very kind of work that they are trained for and most want to do. In fact the gradation is not always as sharp as this. In many areas, we have observed that employing authorities have introduced a post, variously called "area officer" or "senior worker", which combines some of the functions of youth worker and supervising officer. Some authorities avoid the nomenclature of worker or officer altogether. All the same, we think that more recognition should be given to the kind of post which, in the analogous sphere of the social services, is often called "senior practitioner". By this we mean a senior and experienced youth worker who, while continuing to concentrate on the four tasks mentioned earlier, does so on a wider canvas, and combines this role with that of professional supervisor and adviser in relation to other staff. This is one of the ways in which the professional support function, which we consider essential, could be further developed.

9.11   We referred in chapter 8 to the management functions which need to be carried out within the Youth Service. These were concerned with policies— objectives, resources, evaluation and so on; but there is another equally important set of management functions which has to do with personnel. Both these sets of functions are carried out by *youth officers*, on the LEA side and in the voluntary sector. The role is clearly of enormous importance, and the numbers involved are comparatively small—perhaps not more than 1,500 all told.

9.12   Here again the routes into this particular role in the Youth Service are diverse. Some youth officers are drawn from other educational fields, or from cognate field such as the social services, just as some youth workers move off into other fields rather than enter Youth Service management. This again is inevitable, especially where youth provision is on a "youth and community" basis, but it is desirable that senior officers who have to deal with field staff should have had experience and training in the Youth Service.

9.13   There is one feature in the career structure of the Youth Service which differentiates it from some other educational sectors, such as schools or further education. In the Youth Service, officers tend to combine the roles of "administrator" and professional adviser or "organiser". This derives in part from the mixed nature of the youth worker role, and in part from the small numbers of officers, varying from about 25 in some authorities down to 3 or 4 in others. Though in many ways this is a source of strength, it does remove an element of choice within the career structure, and makes it the more necessary for employing authorities to consider seriously the career development of their full- time staff, and to be wary of appointing to senior positions people who do not have Youth Service training and experience.

9.14   One choice which does remain open, at worker and officer level alike, is to work either for a LEA or for a voluntary organisation. The line between the sectors is crossed and re-crossed by many, and it is good that this is so, given what we have said about the structuring of the partnership between authorities and voluntary bodies. As we urged in 8.32, a strong officer team is required on both sides of the line. The voluntary sector will need to do more to develop the officer function (whether performed by paid or unpaid staff) and not to expect LEA officers to perform its own proper administrative tasks; nor should LEAs assume that their own officers can fulfil the administrative needs of the voluntary sector. (See also 10.31).

Part-time staff

9.15   It is difficult, as we have said in 9.2, to be certain about either the total number of part-time staff or the types of job in which they are mostly to be found. What is clear is that the boundary between part-time staff and volunteers is very fluid: it is indeed quite normal for part-time staff to put in more hours on a voluntary basis than they are paid for, and the fact that they are now expected to do so in some areas is a matter for concern. This makes it difficult to pinpoint the precise sphere of the part-timer: it has more to do with the context or setting than with the activity that is being performed. It is often a question of ensuring the carrying out of a function which needs to be done but does not justify a full-time post. Some typical examples of roles performed by part-timers are:

(1) as club leaders in urban or rural areas under the supervision of full-time "area organisers";

(2) as assistants to the full-time club leaders in large city and suburban clubs;

(3) as people brought into a club or centre to organise some particular skilled activity (*e.g.* motor cycle maintenance, judo, dancing, etc.);

(4) as staff trained and experienced in one specific skill—*e.g.* counselling.

9.16   The valuable contribution made by part-timers is often due to the fact that they combine a specific skill with a link with the local community. As Youth Service activities depend more and more on a team approach, the part-timer has an increasingly important part to play. But there are two prerequisites. One—to which we shall return in more detail in 9.45—is training. The other is an appropriately flexible style of management, able to turn to good advantage the varied skills and no less varied periods of time which are on offer. The experienced full-time worker soon learns this, but may encounter obstacles in the shape of management rules and regulations which do not provide the maximum incentive for part-timers to join and remain in the Service.

9.17   The Youth Service is not the only occupation where a mixture of part-time and full-time staff is common: problems arise in other spheres, but the technique of building teams on this basis is well understood. The difficulties which the Youth Service faces, and often succeeds in solving, arise through the mixture of part-time paid staff and volunteers in much the same situation. Careful attention to briefing and supervision is then essential. Part-time work should normally be regarded as carrying with it some obligation to undergo appropriate initial and in-service training, and this can present problems where, for example, suitable training programmes have not been developed, or where a part-timer is already qualified in some other sphere either related to youth work (*e.g.* teaching or social services) or not related at all. Above all the part-timer will need supervision—both management supervision and personal professional support; and it must be accepted as part of the function of the full-time staff to provide this.

Volunteers

9.18   The fact that volunteers form numerically by far the largest group of staff in the Youth Service is, as we have said, one of the most striking features of the Service. There are very few other services which have succeeded in harnessing voluntary manpower as effectively, and few that have even tried. It is worth reflecting for a moment on why the Youth Service is distinguished in this way. Partly of course it is because a main strand of Youth Service provision was conceived on a voluntary basis and has remained true to its first principles. But it is also because the providing authorities in both the statutory and voluntary sectors have made definite efforts to make and keep a place for the volunteer, in all sorts of different ways. Unhappily there seems to be no reason to suppose that this feature is necessarily permanent. Complaints from one area that volunteers are no longer forthcoming are balanced by healthy recruitment in another; and, as one would expect, much depends on the willingness of management and workers to create "space" for the volunteers. But in general we sense a concern in both the LEAs and the voluntary organisations that present circumstances make it increasingly difficult to sustain voluntary effort. Unemployment in particular is an adverse factor: many voluntary organisations believe that it actively deters people from giving their services voluntarily (See 10.20).

9.19 Although in our experience the Youth Service abounds with examples of devoted work by men and women volunteers, including not a few family teams, it should not be thought that this situation just happens. Volunteers do not just come along: they have to be found. They do not just stay: they have to be kept. They do not just get better with experience: they have to be trained. They have also to be able to meet the incidental expenses of being a volunteer, which for some is increasingly difficult. It is therefore essential that volunteers be accorded a status that they value, and are carefully briefed on the role which they have to play.

9.20 It is in the nature of things that there is virtually no role which a volunteer cannot fill, provided that he or she has the requisite background and experience and that the person to whom the volunteer is responsible has recognised these qualities and taken them into account in the briefing. The briefing must include the process of reaching an understanding of the volunteer's limitations, which he or she may not always recognise. This obviously requires great tact and skill on the part of the organiser, qualities which should be possessed by virtue of professional training. Another feature of volunteer work is that as a general rule—there are of course exceptions—the volunteer is not anxious to be tested or deployed in extreme situations, and it is part of the organiser's job to know when this limit has been reached. There are in fact many jobs which volunteers do, in the LEA and voluntary sectors, which are not particularly exacting but nevertheless extremely important, such as fund-raising and support tasks.

9.21 All this means that the handling of a large volunteer force, which is one of the strengths of the Youth Service, is a priority task which itself calls for great skill and a measure of resources in manpower terms. It would be a matter for concern if the full-time force were to become so hard-pressed and reduced in numbers that it could no longer devote time to the recruitment and management of volunteers, especially in adverse economic conditions: in that event the volunteer element would rapidly wither away, and could not easily be revived.

Training for youth work

Present arrangements

9.22 The present pattern of training arrangements dates back to the Albemarle Report, which recommended an emergency scheme of training based on a one-year course for those wishing to take up full-time employment as youth leaders. In 1960 a National College was set up specifically for this purpose. During the next ten years the College trained over a thousand full-time workers, many of whom are still in the Service. Youth leaders were also trained on a two-year course in a voluntary college of education and at one-year courses offered by two voluntary organisations and a university department of education.

9.23   In the later 1960s a strong trend towards longer courses of professional training was making itself felt in many fields, and at the same time the Youth Service began to be seen to have close affinities with other caring occupations. As a result, when the emergency training scheme was brought to an end in 1970, basic courses for youth workers and community centre wardens were established in six existing institutions already concerned with training for related professions (DES Circular 3/70). The new courses were intended to provide two years' full-time training for first posts in youth or community work and also to provide a suitable basis for further training for those who wished later to transfer to other areas of the social or educational services. This set the pattern for the present system in England, which broadly consists of eleven two-year courses and two one-year postgraduate courses. In addition there are two routes to qualification for those who are in post but untrained (a not inconsiderable number as we have seen in 9.8 above): a three-year part-time course at Avery Hill College and a new distance-learning course at the YMCA National College.

9.24   The widening and developing of youth work practice in the course of the last decade has undoubtedly had an effect on the content and curriculum of the present youth work courses, but other influences have also been at work. One of the most potent is the fact that the courses were originally intended to have elements transferable to fields other than youth work, although this did not fully materialise. Another is the fact that, since the early days of the National College, the courses have provided not only a main avenue for entry into the profession of youth work, but also the means of entry to a profession for men and women from skilled and semi-skilled occupations who lack the basic academic qualifications for training for other professions. It has become increasingly common for course staff to see "second-chance" education as one of the functions of their courses. Insofar as it has resulted in considerable flexibility over entry qualifications, this is a good thing and one that deserves full exploitation; but it has led to some uncertainty of purpose.

9.25   Finally, there has never been any consensus, or any means of arriving at a consensus, between trainers and employers on methods and curricula. Each centre goes its own way and, while of course a proper degree of autonomy is essential, the evidence before us suggests far more than the normal degree of tension between trainers and employers. We have met criticisms that the content of the courses often has little relation to work in the field; that there is little agreement on what disciplines should be taught; and that many courses are structured more on what are felt to be the personal developmental needs of the students than on the requirements of the jobs to be performed. As a form of adult or second-chance education and as a broad preparation for working with people, the courses offered are admirable and have involved much exciting pioneering work; and some undoubtedly offer a good preparation for a career in youth work. But there are sources of dissatisfaction which we think need urgently to be explored.

9.26   The training agencies described above are not the only sources of full-time workers. Qualified status as a youth worker is granted to all those who satisfy the requirements of the Secretary of State for the status of qualified teacher. Many in the Youth Service question this arrangement and feel that the recognition of trained teachers as qualified for youth work should be restricted to those who have undertaken courses containing an agreed level of specific youth work training or who have taken appropriate additional training.

9.27   There is also the question of the general option in youth work offered in certain colleges of education. The intention of this option was to combine training for youth work with the normal course of teacher training for a limited number of students. College closures and amalgamations, cuts in the size of student intakes, and reductions in the number of B.Ed courses have led to a drastic curtailment of these youth option courses. The present output is of the order of fifty students a year. Only about 40–60% of these seek Youth Service posts, since many feel the need to complete their probationary period as teachers as quickly as possible; but some may enter youth work later. We would consider the disappearance of these courses as a matter for great regret, and would indeed wish to recommend an increased output, for reasons explained in 9.35 below.

9.28   No suitable body exists at present to exercise judgement on the important issues mentioned so far in this chapter. A national committee—the Joint Negotiating Committee for Youth Leaders and Community Centre Wardens (JNC)—is at present responsible for considering the suitability of qualifications for recognition for qualified status and making recommendations to the Secretary of State. This Committee is also responsible for negotiating salary scales and conditions of service, and its constitution reflects that function, comprising an employers' panel and a staff panel. It is the only body at present which can act as a national accrediting body, although it is not fully satisfactory for this purpose since it lacks systematic machinery for assessing the courses which it accepts as according qualified status for youth workers.

Critical issues raised in evidence

9.29   It is clear from this brief sketch of present arrangements, which reflects important strands in the evidence we have received, that there are many issues in the field of training for youth work which call for critical study and evaluation. The list is too long for us to go into any detail, but the principal elements are as follows:

(1)   the content of training and its relationship with practice;

(2)   clarification of the routes to qualification;

(3)   review of probation procedures;

(4)   development of in-service training (and its relationship to probation);

(5)   training for management and the training of trainers;

(6)   consideration of the need for a practice-related qualification;

(7)   the establishment of a supervisory body to monitor and co-ordinate both initial and in-service training, and to control professional registration;

(8)   financial support for those in training;

(9)   training of part-time and volunteer staff.

We do not consider ourselves properly constituted to investigate all these questions. On some of them we have formed views which we set out below, and on one of them we wish to make a firm recommendation. Since this recommendation provides the key to much of what follows, and since it appears that progress is already being made along lines which we approve, we will deal with it first.

A national supervisory body

9.30   On no aspect of training has there been a greater measure of unanimity, in the evidence submitted to us, than on the need for a suitably constituted national body to monitor and supervise courses of initial training. For in-service training such a function is performed at least in part by the In-Service Training and Education Panel (INSTEP) established in 1976 by the DES, but for initial training there has never been a body with the necessary authority and competence. We believe that it is essential that there should be a single body capable of endorsing and monitoring courses of both initial and in-service training for youth and community work. The essential responsibility of such a body would be to maintain professional standards, and we see this as involving the following tasks:

(1) assessing and endorsing courses against published guidelines and criteria;

(2) exercising a continuing surveillance involving regular reviews of accredited courses;

(3) regulating standards of entry to courses;

(4) investigating the need for new curriculum developments in the light of changing requirements;

(5) in cases of individual recognition, assessing particular courses against agreed criteria; and

(6) reviewing the distribution and volume of training facilities in relation to employment needs.

9.31   Since we first formed this view we have noted that developments are under way which would go a long way towards meeting these requirements. The DES has taken the initiative of inviting INSTEP to prepare proposals for the enlargement of its functions to include the professional endorsement of courses of initial training. The proposals which are understood to be under consideration appear to involve the establishment under one reorganised panel of two committees, one for initial training and the other for in-service training, both composed of representatives of employers, staff associations, training agencies, and the Joint Negotiating Committee.

9.32   This development appears to us to be on the right lines. It is not clear at the time of writing this report what the precise remit and authority of the new panel would be; but details which have so far emerged encourage the hope that there will soon appear a body capable of giving proper consideration to many of the key issues which we have identified above. We deal with some of these in more detail below, more in order to indicate what needs to be considered than to make firm recommendations. There is, however, one point which needs to be made about the remit and constitution of the panel. It concerns its relationship to the national body which we have recommended in the previous chapter.

9.33 The new panel will be concerned with the nature, quality and extent of education and training available for those seeking qualified status and for all full-time personnel in the Youth Service. It does not appear to us possible to keep these matters under review without referring back to the aims and objectives of the Service and the needs of young people which it seeks to fulfil. These are the province of our proposed advisory council on youth affairs (8.10) and we therefore think that the link between the two bodies should be appropriately recognised. This might be arranged by including amongst the representatives on the panel itself (though not necessarily on either of its committees) a representative of the advisory council.

Routes to qualification

9.34 It would seem to us appropriate that the job of maintaining a register of people qualified for youth work should be taken over by the new panel. It is to be hoped that this will lead to a review of the whole process of career development and clarification of the routes to qualification. We must at this point say something about the position of qualified teachers. As we have said in 9.26, qualified teacher status is apparently taken to imply automatic qualification for youth work. This assumption no longer seems acceptable, particularly since the teacher training courses with youth options (referred to in 9.27 above) have declined. It should be one of the tasks of the new panel to examine this matter. In general we would consider that the recognition of a teacher as qualified for youth work would depend on having taken, or undertaking to go through, a relevant course of training. This question needs study as much from the supply angle as from that of career development.

9.35 With regard to the youth option courses, which we understand to be currently under review, we would recommend an expansion for three reasons. First, if qualified teachers ceased to be automatically accepted as qualified youth workers, a supply problem might arise unless there were more teachers with the double qualification. Secondly, these courses are the main source of staff eligible for joint teacher/youth worker appointments. The total number of such posts is not easily ascertainable: they probably amount to about 20% of the total full-time manpower in the Youth Service, and where they occur they tend to be posts of special importance and responsibility. Yet the reduction in the number of youth option courses has meant that increasingly these posts are filled by people who have had no initial training relevant to the work they do. Finally, we have repeatedly emphasised the need for cognate services to keep in touch. A common recognition of need and a common approach is beginning to emerge in the Youth Service, schools and colleges, projects funded by the Manpower Services Commission and some social services activities, and others. A course which recognises the affinities in two adjoining fields seems to us to deserve increased support for that reason alone.

97

Content of training

9.36 It is to be expected that the new panel will give urgent attention to the content and direction of the training curriculum in initial courses. What seems to be needed is not a detailed and meticulous attempt to control every aspect of the curriculum—it is right that the training agencies should have a proper measure of academic and professional freedom—but a greater degree of consensus between agencies and employers about the broad aim of the courses. A recapitulation of some of the criticisms expressed about the courses will serve to illustrate the directions in which further study and discussion are needed.

(1) The lack of clarity about the aims of youth work has hindered good curriculum development. (This reinforces the need for the national advisory council which we have recommended in chapter 8 to be represented on the panel).

(2) Those courses which have a more experimental approach are criticised by employers for not training students to fill available jobs in the Youth Service.

(3) Those courses which are more traditional still do not prepare students for the fourfold role outlined at the beginning of this chapter.

(4) The concept of "youth and community" has resulted in courses which do not train students for placement in the Youth Service at all.

Probation procedures

9.37 According to the conditions laid down by the JNC, the first year in post of a full-time worker after training should be seen as a probationary year. Probation—as opposed to induction or familiarisation with any new job—is a concept which probably does need clarification. Not all professions have arrangements for it: for example, social workers do not, whereas teachers do. On the whole the balance of the evidence which we have received is in favour of retaining the concept of probation but giving it a more positive meaning. This means viewing it as essentially a continuation of the process of professional development in a structured way. The methods of helping workers to make the best use of the probationary year are, broadly speaking, those of in-service training, professional supervision, and assessment. Guidelines need to be laid down with these objectives in mind.

Professional support and supervision

9.38 We have referred in the earlier half of this chapter to the need for effective machinery which allows the full-time worker (and also the part-timer and the volunteer) to discuss problems with a sympathetic and experienced fellow professional who is not necessarily his or her line manager. Supervision in this special sense can be provided in various ways, *e.g.* by special relationships between established staff, through paid consultants, or through specially constituted support groups. In our view not enough priority is given to this provision, which is highly necessary wherever staff are involved in demanding personal relationships with their clients. A study of existing methods is desirable.

In-service training

9.39 We see in-service training as a general process, beginning during the probationary year, but continuing throughout the professional career of the youth worker and youth officer, sometimes intermittently, sometimes in more intensive spells—*e.g.* when major policy developments (such as the Government's proposed new Youth Training Scheme) are taking place, or following upon a change in activity or status (as from worker to officer). The major initiative by the DES and the trainers in setting up INSTEP has laid a good foundation and is beginning to show results; but progress and resources seem slow to appear, and more fundamentally the current stance of INSTEP is mainly a reactive one. Its role appears largely to be that of approving courses presented to it by others. We would see the new panel as playing a much more initiatory role, giving a lead in proposing the kinds of programme which full-time staff will need in the light of the developing service. Areas in which training still needs to be developed include:

(1) general supplementary courses for youth workers with one year of post-Albemarle training;

(2) conversion courses for teachers, social workers and others;

(3) courses for current and prospective youth officers: a beginning has been made in certain regions with courses for newly appointed officers, but these need to be much more widely spread. There is also a need for refresher courses and specialist courses for officers already in post;

(4) courses in specific skills, *e.g.* counselling, supervision, management techniques for youth workers, self-evaluation;

(5) courses in training for those with training responsibilities in the Youth Service;

(6) updating courses in new or emerging features in the Youth Service—*e.g.* work on combating racism and work with multi-ethnic communities, work with girls, work with the unemployed and new initiatives in encouraging young people to organise their own activities.

This list could be extended: we have only mentioned items which seem to us of outstanding importance.

Need for a practice-related further qualification

9.40 We have indicated above that in our view the process of professional development is a continuous one, interspersed with periods of further study and training. It has been represented to us that there is a desire amongst workers and officers for a qualification additional to the initial qualification. Some take degree courses for this purpose, but many would prefer a qualification related to practice. It has been argued that such an award would act as an incentive for people to stay on as workers within the Service rather than look for advancement elsewhere. It might also encourage the wider adoption of the nomenclature and concept of a post of "senior practitioner" to which we have referred in 9.10. There seems to us to be merit in this idea, and we hope that the new panel will give it early consideration.

Supply considerations

9.41 All the tasks for the new panel which we have considered so far are related to the processes of training and professional development. There is, however, another area of study which we do not think can be omitted from the panel's terms of reference. This is the whole question of supply and demand as distinct from training. The two sets of considerations are not, in our view, truly separable, since if the training processes are to be more closely geared to the real needs of the Youth Service, then consideration will have to be given both to the nature and extent of those needs and to the required capacity of the training plant and its distribution across the country. No doubt the final arbiter in the matter of supply must be the Secretary of State, but he will need expert advice.

9.42   For sound advice to be available it seems essential that both the training panel and the national advisory council (recommended in 8.10) should be involved. We have already referred (in 9.33) to the need for links between the two. Since the one would be representative of outside organisations and the other not, the relationship should not be too rigid; but in general we would expect the advisory council to offer advice on broad staffing needs in relation to the aims, objectives and performance of the Youth Service, while the panel would bring to bear detailed knowledge of the training plant and expertise in curriculum development.

Mandatory grants for students

9.43   The relationship between training and supply has a bearing on yet another topic which, though not strictly within the remit of the new panel, would reinforce the need for it to keep supply considerations within its sights. From many quarters we have had urgent representations that the grants available for the support of trainees on full-time courses of initial training should be mandatory and not, as now, discretionary. If the Youth Service is placed on a firm statutory footing, as we recommend (in chapter 11), and as a career in it becomes properly structured and conditioned by appropriate training and development processes, then the case for mandatory grants becomes in our view very strong. A particular reason for introducing this change has to do with a number of people who wish to train for the Youth Service later in life, after they have pursued some other occupation, without having any paper qualifications. These are often the most valuable recruits to the Service; yet time and again we have been told that they encounter difficulty in obtaining discretionary awards.

9.44   We understand that it is within the power of the Secretary of State to designate appropriate courses as eligible for mandatory grants, and we recommend that full-length courses of training in youth work be added to this list. We recognise that there would be difficulty in the case of those who had already undergone with grant assistance training in some other occupation. We would not like these to be lost either, and the solution may lie in developing for them shorter forms of initial training. So long as this shorter period did not exceed one year, it might be possible to consider making mandatory awards available for these shorter courses even though the recipients had had earlier grants. We appreciate that all this will make it the more necessary to keep control over the input and output of courses, and we therefore see it as a further reason why the proposed new national supervisory panel should concern itself with supply considerations.

Training of part-time and volunteer staff

9.45   We turn now to a different field of training for the Youth Service which we do not see as one of the responsibilities of the proposed panel though it may have a part to play. This is the question of training for the huge numbers of part-time staff and volunteers who, as we have seen, play such a crucial part in the Service.

9.46   Training programmes for voluntary workers may be said to have been pioneered by certain of the voluntary organisations, particularly the uniformed bodies. Development took place mainly along the lines of weekend courses backed up by assessment of practice, and was naturally related specifically to the methods, objectives and programmes of the bodies concerned. Undoubtedly there is an impressive store of expertise underlying such training programmes.

9.47   Other providing bodies, including some LEAs, had also made an early start in this field, and a bid was made in the report of a working party under Mr Gordon Bessey* published in 1962 to pool and share this experience. This report called for full consultation and co-operation between LEA and voluntary partners; for the establishment of training committees jointly by the two sectors; and also for local joint training agencies for the training of trainers. It indicated minimum standards and suggested a common element in LEA and voluntary body training programmes.

9.48   For a time these objectives were to some extent realised, progress being marked by a second report issued by the Youth Service Department Council in 1966†; but there has been some falling back. The full pooling of expertise sought by the Bessey Working Party has never really borne fruit, although most LEAs now conduct training for part-time workers and volunteers in one form or another and many have developed elaborate programmes which involve some sections at least of the voluntary sector. Joint training committees still exist in some areas, but few have had the degree of success once hoped for. The late 1960s and early 1970s saw the experimental emergence of a number of joint training agencies, but these have mostly disappeared, partly as a result of local government reorganisation and expenditure cuts, but also and more fundamentally because significant groups within the voluntary sector felt that their particular ethos and style of delivery called for training programmes specific to them and organised on a national rather than a local basis. Regional Advisory Councils have played a useful though limited role, but not all of them have been as active as they might have been in sponsoring, stimulating and co-ordinating local initiatives: at least one has recently disbanded its Youth Panel.

9.49   We agree therefore with the point which has been made from many quarters that a fresh initiative in this important field is long overdue. It is probably not appropriate, however, to attempt to resurrect the Bessey concept

---

* 'The Training of Part-time Youth Leaders and Assistants: Report of the Working Party appointed by the Minister of Education in July 1961' (London HMSO, 1962).
† 'A Second Report on the Training of Part-time Youth Leaders and Assistants: Report of the Review Committee of the Youth Service Development Council, December 1965' (London, HMSO, 1966).

of common-element training: there may be certain modes of youth work where there is sufficient commonality for this approach to yield dividends (*e.g.* in LEA and voluntary club work), but in general it does not seem a fruitful starting point.

9.50   It seems better to start from the situation on the ground, and to recognise that, while the big national voluntary youth organisations will continue to organise their own training programmes for their part-timers and volunteers, most LEAs either separately or in consortia have developed a training capability based on their own local needs, often in collaboration with the local training agency. Locally based voluntary bodies are free to avail themselves of these systems, and many do. What seems to be required is some system for monitoring and moderating these local systems so as to bring about a measure of mutual recognition and interchangeability. It is our firm belief (subject to what we say in 9.51 below) that this could not be brought about in any effective way by a national body. We part company here with some of the bodies who have made suggestions to us. It seems to us that the range of legitimate variation is too great and the sheer volume of administrative work involved would be too fearsome. It could well be, however, that the Regional Advisory Councils could undertake this moderating role effectively, and we recommend that they do so.

9.51   It may be that there are some national guidelines which could be laid down. Proposals to this effect have recently been considered by the Consultative Group on Youth and Community Work Training, a national body of training interests serviced by the National Youth Bureau, and we understand that a small panel of a non-representative nature but compromising a range of relevant expertise has been set up to reivew training needs and to evaluate current trends. No doubt the results will in due course be brought to the attention of all the parties concerned, including the Regional Advisory Councils and the new panel recommended in 9.30–9.33 above.

9.52   Two final comments may be made before we leave the topic of training for part-timers and volunteers. First, the need for professional supervision is certainly no less in their case than it is for full-time workers, though the requirements may be different and capable of being met by suitable full-time staff. Secondly, more experienced part-time and volunteer staff continue to need in-service training appropriate to the level of their increasing skill and expertise, to develop management ability and to keep abreast of new developments in youth culture and the Youth Service. Often the requirements are not dissimilar to those of full-time staff and, wherever possible, in-service training should be arranged jointly for full-time, part-time and volunteer workers.

9.53   *Summary of recommendations*

   (1) Workers should accept as essential parts of their work both managerial work, involving personnel work and administration, and face-to-face work, involving work with young people and community development. These four functions should be reflected in their training. (9.1)

   (2) More needs to be done to correct the balance of representation of

women and ethnic minorities, especially amongst full-time workers and at officer level. (9.4—9.5)

(3) Management should give thought to finding means of easing the problem of maintaining morale among full-time workers in a small and open-ended service, *e.g.* by facilitating transfers and by extending the career structure. (9.9—9.10)

(4) Part-timers provide special skills and links with the local community, and have special briefing and supervision needs. (9.16—9.17)

(5) Volunteers are a special feature of the Youth Service but their contribution cannot be taken for granted. Special efforts have to be made to recruit and retain them. (9.18—9.21)

(6) There is a clear and urgent need for a national supervisory panel to accredit and monitor both initial and in-service training for full-time staff. It should be concerned with supply as well as training. (9.30)

(7) Consideration should be given to the acceptance of qualified teachers as qualified youth workers only after an assessment of the training they have undertaken or are prepared to take. The youth option in B Ed courses should be developed and expanded. (9.34—9.35)

(8) Urgent consideration should be given to the development of many areas of probation, professional support and in-service training. (9.37—9.40)

(9) Mandatory grants should be available for those undertaking a course of initial training for the Youth Service. (9.43—9.44)

(10) Training programmes for part-time staff and volunteers should continue to be developed on a local basis, but a moderating and co-ordinating role should be undertaken by Regional Advisory Councils. (9.50)

CHAPTER 10: RESOURCES

Lack of reliable data. Total volume of resources available to the Youth Service, including the voluntary sector. Local authority provision: expenditure since 1970; numbers of full-time youth workers, part-time workers and youth officers; availability of central public funds in addition to RSG. Voluntary provision: expansion during 1970s. Emerging needs; effectiveness of existing uses of resources. Implications for local authorities, voluntary bodies, and the DES.

10.1   In this chapter we consider the resources that are available to the Youth Service for the various forms of provision which we have discussed earlier. We have, however, encountered difficulty in trying to assess the total amount of such resources and their distribution. Some basic data are lacking, and the information which does exist, particularly in the field of staffing, often appears contradictory. Reconciling conflicting evidence has not been easy because the different sources may cover only one part of the field and, for various reasons, be inconsistent in themselves and not wholly accurate. Our first recommendation in this chapter must therefore be that comprehensive statistics should be kept on a reliable, consistent and comparable basis for each sector of the Service. We consider that this might be a job for the National Youth Bureau because of its declared aim of acting as a national resource centre for information about the Youth Service. In suggesting that basic statistics should be compiled by the same body for both sectors, we do not mean to imply that voluntary resources should be co-ordinated with statutory resources. This would be contrary to the spirit of voluntaryism. Nevertheless, those who are responsible for policy-making and review must have adequate statistics for the whole range of the Service if they are to carry out their task effectively.

10.2   Despite the difficulties involved, we have been able to draw on various sources of information. Financial and staffing data have been made available by the DES, and further details for the statutory sector have been obtained from publications of the Chartered Institute of Public Finance and Accountancy (CIPFA). This information has been brought up to date for 1981–82 through local authority responses to the questionnaire which we sent out at the start of our work. In addition, the National Council for Voluntary Youth Services (NCVYS) has supplied estimates of resources in the voluntary sector. All this statistical information has been supplemented by the informal views of HM Inspectorate and by impressions gained from the field, in evidence submitted to us and on our visits around the country.

Total resources

10.3   In order to estimate the total amount of resources available to the Youth Service, it is not enough to look simply at local authorities' Youth Service budgets. Even in the statutory sector, the real amount of resources absorbed is much more than the £80m or so a year identified in local authorities' recent accounts as expenditure on the Service. (See 10.8 below.) In many areas the Service also benefits, to an unquantifiable extent, from other local authority expenditure, *e.g.* on schools, further and adult education, leisure and recreation, and social services, largely through the subsidised use of premises and equipment. (See 10.6 below.) In addition, voluntary resources flow into the statutory sector through financial contributions in the form of subscriptions, sales, fund-raising, loans, gifts and so forth from club members, parents and the community at large. Evidence from a number of authorities indicates that this may be equivalent on average to about 25% of their net recurrent expenditure on the Youth Service.

10.4   The voluntary sector also has access to finances which are considerable, though difficult to gauge precisely. NCVYS has estimated, on the basis of figures available to it from its constituent organisations, that there are 100,000–140,000 units in the voluntary sector and that the average cost of maintaining each unit is currently £2,000–£4,000 a year. If these estimates are likely, the voluntary sector must be able to draw on funds of at least £200m a year. Within the sector, however, voluntary aided organisations should be distinguished from independent ones. The former benefit from local authority grants, which have already been accounted for by local authority expenditure; but, while the grants may be the major source of funding for an individual organisation, they probably form only a small proportion of total voluntary sector funds. The majority comes from trusts (particularly the Royal Jubilee Trusts, but also innumerable local trusts), settlements, gifts, investments, fund-raising, subscriptions, central government grants and so on.

10.5   Over and above these funds is the help given to both sectors by volunteers. The extent of this resource is almost impossible to quantify, but we have reckoned that there may be as many as half a million volunteers in the Service. On the minimal assumption that each volunteer worked one evening a week for 50 weeks in the year and that this were remunerated at £5 an hour, the total amount of all these volunteers' work would be worth £500m a year. The reality is a great deal more, as many volunteers work more than one evening a week. Many paid workers also give time freely; part-time staff may work for up to half as many hours again as they are paid for, and undertake training in their own time.

10.6   We have already mentioned (in 10.3 above) another unquantifiable resource which is of benefit to both sectors—access to premises and equipment maintained by various departments within local authorities. Organisations in the statutory sector may have the use of schools, other educational premises and sports and leisure facilities, as well as their own accommodation. Many of these are available to voluntary youth organisations as well, often through a system of registration or affiliation. At least one third of all authorities offer such organisations the use of premises free of charge. Others provide them at subsidised letting rates. There is evidence that some authorities have recently increased their charges (see 10.22 below), but it happens rarely, if ever, that a full-cost charge is made. This is a particularly valuable form of assistance, without which many organisations might find it difficult to operate.

10.7   Putting together all these resource elements—the voluntary contributions flowing into the statutory sector, the maintenance costs in the voluntary sector, the work carried out by volunteers in both sectors, and the unquantifiable amount represented by the subsidised use of premises and equipment—we estimate that the indicated expenditure by local education authorities would need to be increased by at least an order of magnitude to give some idea of the level of activity in the statutory and voluntary sectors put together; and that the sum total of resources is therefore of the order of about £1,000 million. This is not a reason for complacency. Although the local authority contribution constitutes only a small part of the Service's total resources, it is the keystone which provides strategic support for the voluntary initiatives which sustain the wider edifice. It would be wrong to assume that if local authority support were reduced, new voluntary effort would take up the slack: on the contrary, much of the current voluntary provision would fall.

Provision made or assisted by local authorities

10.8   Table 1 below gives more detail about the provision made or assisted by local authorities. It shows that net recurrent expenditure by authorities on the Youth Service increased in real terms during the 1970s by £28m or 53%, from £53m in 1970–71 to £81m in 1979–80 (at November 1980 prices). The rate of increase was most rapid in the early 1970s (annual average value about 6%), but it continued at a fairly steady, if lower, level during the later part of the decade (annual average increase about 4%). Only in the last financial year for which actual figures are available, 1980–81, has there been a reduction in expenditure in real terms, by 4% on the 1979–80 figure. Nevertheless, at £78m, the 1980–81 figure is still £25m more or 47% higher than that for 1970–71.

TABLE 1

Local Authority Net Recurrent Expenditure on the Youth Service

Financial Year	Out-turn Prices	Constant Prices*	As a proportion of total LEA net recurrent expenditure on education	Per head of 11–18 year old population*
	£m	£m	%	£
1970–71	12	53	0.86	10.4
1971–72	15	58	0.88	11.0
1972–73	18	63	0.89	11.7
1973–74	22	67	0.87	12.3
1974–75	27	67	0.85	12.0
1975–76	37	70	0.88	12.2
1976–77	43	71	0.86	12.1
1977–78	48	74	0.92	12.5
1978–79	53	77	0.94	12.8
1979–80	65	81	0.99	13.4
1980–81	78	78	0.98	12.9

* At November 1980 prices.
England only.
Sources: Local authority returns on Form RO1 of recurrent expenditure on education.
         GAD mid-year population estimates.

10.9　Table 1 also shows that there has been an increase in expenditure on the Youth Service compared with other areas of education in the maintained sector during the 1970s. The proportion of total local authority net recurrent expenditure on education devoted to the Service rose from 0.86% in 1970–71 to 0.99% in 1979–80, with only a marginal drop in 1980–81 to 0.98%. Most of the increase took place in the later 1970s. In other words, whilst there was a slowing down in the rate of absolute increase in net recurrent expenditure on the Youth Service in the later 1970s, the Service fared comparatively better than other parts of the maintained sector and took a larger share of total expenditure. This share is, however, still only about 1%.

10.10　At the same time as local authority net recurrent expenditure on the Service has been rising, the size of the relevant age-group has also been increasing. The 11–18 age-group may provide an approximation for this: during the 1970s it is estimated to have risen by 18% from 5.1m to just over 6m. Expenditure has, nevertheless, been rising more rapidly, as is reflected in the increase in expenditure per head of the 11–18 population by 29% from about £10.40 in 1970–71 to about £13.40 in 1979–80 (at constant prices). Again, 1980–81 showed a decline on the latter figure to about £12.90, but this is still 24% higher than the 1970–71 figure.

10.11　In both absolute and relative terms, therefore, the 1970s saw an increase in local authority expenditure on the Youth Service, while the 1980s seem to have brought the beginning of retrenchment. We now consider what these overall figures mean in terms of manpower resources available to the Service. The picture here is confused. One source of evidence is expenditure on salaries, which forms the largest single item within total authority net recurrent expenditure on the Service. Table 2 overleaf shows that this rose by 70% during the 1970s. The rate of increase was again higher during the first part of the decade, when the average annual increase was 8% compared with 4% in the later 1970s. The overall increase was more rapid than that in overall expenditure on the Youth Service, particularly after 1973–74: hence its share of the total has increased from 57% in 1970–71 to 65% in 1980–81. Since 1978–79, however, expenditure on salaries has remained almost static, both absolutely and compared with other expenditure on the Service.

10.12　The long-term increase in salary expenditure is, however, obviously due partly to higher salary costs in real terms as well as to a growth in the number of Youth Service staff employed by local authorities. To identify the latter more precisely, it is necessary to turn to other sources of information on staffing. Unfortunately, none of these provides comprehensive data; nor are they necessarily comparable. The DES Register of Youth Workers and Community Centre Wardens, which covers full-time workers only but includes those employed by both statutory and voluntary bodies, shows numbers steadily increasing through the 1970s. Table 3. This picture of growth seems to be borne out by grossed-up staffing totals from our own questionnaire, which place the number of full-time workers employed or supported by authorities at about 3,500 in 1981.

10.13　CIPFA figures, on the other hand, indicate a decline in the number of full-time-equivalent workers employed by authorities since the mid-70s, and

TABLE 2

Local Authority Expenditure on Youth Service Salaries

Financial Year	Out-turn Prices £m	Constant Prices* £m	As a proportion of LEA net recurrent expenditure on the Youth Service* %
1970–71	7	30	57
1971–72	9	33	57
1972–73	11	38	60
1973–74	13	39	58
1974–75	17	41	61
1975–76	24	45	64
1976–77	28	46	65
1977–78	30	47	64
1978–79	35	51	66
1979–80	40	50	62
1980–81	51	51	65

* at November 1980 prices.
England only.
Source: Local authority returns on Form RO1 of recurrent expenditure on education.

TABLE 3

Full-time Youth Workers and Community Centre Wardens

1970	2,100*
1974	2,500*
1978	2,900

* estimate based on England and Wales figure.
England only.
Source: DES Register of full-time Youth Workers and Community Centre Wardens.
(Although figures have been compiled for intervening years, only those for the years in which full censuses were carried out—1970, 1974, 1978—appear to be reliable).

particularly between 1976–77 and 1977–78 and again, to a lesser extent, between 1980–81 and 1981–82. Table 4. Although these figures are only forward estimates, the downward trend is confirmed by the views of those in the field that staffing numbers have been declining for some years. The apparent contradiction between this conclusion and the impression gained from the DES Register and increasing salary expenditure may, in our view, be explained by the likelihood that, while resources have gone to keeping the number of full-time workers up, a decline in overall staffing has taken place and has been concentrated on part-time workers and officers. Views from the field confirm that between 1976–77 and 1977–78 there was a sharp reduction in part-time numbers, which extended to those grant-aided in the voluntary sector as well as those employed by authorities. With a few exceptions, such as the East Midlands, where staffing held its ground or even recovered, the decline in officer numbers and part-time hours continued between 1977 and 1980; and all agree that 1981–82 has seen further cuts in numbers. This gives us grounds for anxiety, although we recognise that authorities may have sought to reduce staffing numbers in a way least harmful to the Service.

TABLE 4

Full-time Equivalent Youth Wardens and Leaders

1976–77	5,600*
1977–78	4,790
1978–79	4,850
1979–80	4,730
1980–81	4,790
1981–82	4,480

*excluding Richmond-upon-Thames.
England only.
Source: Education Statistics Estimates published by CIPFA (rounded).

10.14   The effect of the reduction in part-time hours seems, however, to have been mitigated by increased voluntary work. We have received evidence from the field that some part-time workers have continued to work the same hours after their number of paid hours has been reduced. This testifies to the commitment of many of those working in the Service. The reduction in paid part-time work has, nevertheless, led to some loss of provision. The decline in officer numbers has also apparently resulted in a deterioration in the Service. Reduced administrative support seems to have led to workers' spending more time on routine office-work and fund-raising and less on work with young people, particularly in innovative areas. It has also resulted in poorer co-ordination and management control.

10.15   Two other relatively recent developments should be noted. First, alongside the decline in staff funded by authorities, there has been a growth in associated personnel working with young people but funded by the Manpower Services Commission. Some of these workers have had experience in the Youth Service, but essentially they are carrying out work which the latter would not normally undertake.

10.16   Secondly, in addition to the Rate Support Grant, there are other central public funds on which authorities can draw to finance the Youth Service, e.g. the Urban Programme, grants made under Section 11 of the Local Government Act 1966, and grants from the Sports and Arts Councils and the British Council. There is evidence that over the last few years a small but increasing amount of Youth Service provision has been financed through, in particular, the Urban Programme, although not all authorities claim or obtain such aid and those that benefit do so to varying extents. Extra funds and staff are no doubt to be

109

welcomed, but the way in which these have entered the Service has brought several problems.

10.17   First, there is the danger of unbalanced and ill-managed provision which results from resources being deployed in a way that escapes the policy-making network and monitoring procedures of the local authority department responsible for the Youth Service. This means that club work has tended to suffer, not so such through clubs being closed as through deteriorating management and supervision, a decline in innovative activities or an over-concentration on sheer numbers. Project work has sometimes been started up without adequate policy studies or sound follow-up practices. Some new activities have been funded with sudden, short-term grants of money and have failed to achieve good results, while well-established activities have languished for lack of funds. When, moreover, these extra resources come to an end, the projects they have been supporting may have to be sustained at the expense of mainline activities, thus distorting the fabric of Youth Service provision.

10.18   Secondly, the availability of funds outside the Rate Support Grant for specific purposes has increased the inequalities of provision that already existed. The range among authorities in rates of expenditure on the Youth Service in 1979–80 and 1980–81 was considerable. At the extreme, expenditure per head of the 11–18 year old population ranged from £2–£41 in 1979–80 and £3–£52 in 1980–81 (at out-turn prices). Discounting a few authorities at either extreme, most fell into the range of £6–£30 each year. Details of budgeted expenditure for the Service provided by authorities (about three-quarters of the total in England) in response to a questionnaire indicated that the range of expenditure might be even greater in 1981–82, i.e. between £4 and £94 per head of the 11–18 population, although most would again be spending between £6 and £30. Some allowance must, of course, be made for the varying needs of different areas; but notional grant-related expenditure (GRE) assessments* for the Youth Service which attempt to do this span a much narrower range, e.g. for 1981–82, £9–£24 per head of the 11–18 population at the extreme, but £11–£20 for all but a handful of authorities. The divergencies in budgeted expenditure from this range essentially reflect the differing priorities accorded by authorities to the Service, as well as their differing overall expenditure policies. We do not wish to suggest that there should be standardised rates of expenditure across the country in place of the current flexibility to meet local needs in the light of local circumstances. Nevertheless, we feel that the wide range in expenditure is leading to a growing and unacceptable disparity in the level and quality of provision between authorities, and even between areas within the same authority. We have seen for ourselves how some areas already well favoured with facilities are maintaining or even increasing these, whilst some poorly endowed areas are losing much of the little provision they had. Our evidence confirms this picture and suggests that the influx of outside resources to the Service in some areas but not others has contributed to increasing inequalities of provision across the country.

---

*For GRE purposes, the Youth Service is linked with other education services and research, which comprise some related facilities, such as community centres, village halls and outdoor pursuit centres, as well as educational research and some miscellaneous items. To arrive at notional figures for the Youth Service, we have deducted 25%.

Voluntary provision

10.19   We have found no way of carrying out a comparable analysis of how resources in the voluntary sector have changed during the last decade. The best indication we have obtained is membership and participant figures for certain national voluntary youth organisations, such as those quoted in 'Social Trends 12'* for the United Kingdom as a whole. Only 14 out of about 50 national voluntary youth organisations are covered by these figures, but we believe that they provide a good indication of the overall growth in voluntary provision. Notwithstanding a decline in some of these 14 organisations, overall membership or participation in their activities has increased by almost 30% over the last decade from almost 2.4m in 1971 to 3.1m in 1980. The growth in membership has proportionately out-stripped the increase in the size of the relevant age-group: the number of 5–20-year-olds in the UK has grown by only about 5% in the same period.

10.20   This impressive growth in membership implies a considerable increase in the resources available to the voluntary sector during the 1970s. There are signs, however, that voluntary organisations are now encountering constraints which are limiting further growth or even resulting in contraction. First, the current recession and lower standards of living for many have made it more difficult for voluntary bodies to raise funds and have resulted in a decline in the number of volunteers in the Service. It is sometimes thought that unemployment results in more unpaid activity being undertaken in the service of the community as those without jobs seek to fill their time in voluntary work. Evidence from the field suggests the contrary. Unemployment tends to discourage voluntary service, partly through its effect on morale and partly because those who undertake voluntary work whilst in regular employment may well take on part-time jobs when made redundant. The working hours required in these jobs may be incompatible with youth work. Unemployment may also cause people to be unable to afford the incidental personal expenditure that voluntary work often implies.

10.21   Secondly, the capital building projects of local voluntary youth organisations has fallen off markedly in recent years. Until 1980 voluntary organisations could apply through their LEA for capital grants from the DES. Typically, the Department would meet 50% of the cost of an approved budget, the LEA 25% and the voluntary organisation the remaining 25%. Table 5 shows that the total sum allocated by the Department in capital grants decreased by about 45% in real terms between 1975–76 and 1980–81. Table 5. There is reason to suppose that the decline has continued since 1980–81. The DES has made no direct allocations of grant for new projects but has transferred funding to the Rate Support Grant. Since no part of the RSG can be earmarked for specific purposes, however, there can be no guarantee that funds are reaching local voluntary organisations in every area. Local authority responses to our questionnaire indicate that for 1981–82 about one-third had decided to take over the former DES capital grant and meet 75% of the cost of approved schemes (sometimes in conjunction with district councils). A few others had

* 'Social Trends 12' (HMSO 1981)

111

increased their level of support to 50%. Some of these authorities had, however, set a limit on the funds available for such support, and others were planning to review their arrangements in the light of their deteriorating financial position. The largest category of authorities, about one half, had made no change in policy or were still reviewing their arrangements. Almost one in ten offered no grants at all and, perhaps most worrying of all, almost a further one in ten had received virtually no applications. This suggests cause for concern over the long-term health of voluntary provision in certain areas.

TABLE 5

DES Capital Grant Allocations to LEAs for Local Voluntary Youth Organsations

Financial Year	Out-turn Prices £m	Constant Prices* £m
1975–76	1.32	2.50
1976–77	1.01	1.68
1977–78	1.31	2.01
1978–79	1.46	2.11
1979–80	1.56	1.94
1980–81	1.36	1.36

* November 1980 prices
England only
Source: DES

10.22   The alternative to building premises is hiring accommodation. There is evidence from the field, however, that charges for hiring some local authority premises, which accommodate so much of even the voluntary Youth Service, have recently risen, although many are still available free of charge. There is a danger that financial pressures on authorities may lead to further increases. Although authorities may still be subsidising the use of premises at no little expense, some voluntary organisations may nevertheless find that they can ill afford the increased charges.

10.23   The net result of all these constraints on the voluntary sector has been a reduction not so much in the number of clubs or organisations as in the volume of their activity.

Emerging needs

10.24   There is little doubt therefore that, after the rapid growth of the 1970s, resources will be under constraint in the 1980s. In this circumstance, the temptation will be to do no more than maintain existing provision as far as possible. As we have shown earlier, however, the Youth Service is in a unique position to help meet the needs of a society which is currently undergoing change. To do this, there must be scope for experiment and innovation. In particular, resources should be available to develop work in the areas of urgent

112

need which we have outlined in chapter 6. These include work to counter urban deprivation, rural isolation and racism; full involvement in training schemes for the employed and unemployed alike; more opportunities for girls; and measures to integrate the handicapped.

10.25 We are bound to admit, however, that we have found no method of establishing whether current resources are sufficient to meet needs. We recognise that, on the one hand, the changing demands being placed on the Service and, on the other, the overall scale, disparate nature and partly voluntary aspect of its resources make evaluation difficult. We nevertheless consider it a shortcoming of the Service that machinery does not exist to monitor the effectiveness of the current use of resources. We recommend that such machinery should be brought into existence as part of the local and national structures discussed in chapter 8. For the meantime, we can make only general recommendations. First, the Youth Service is worth funding at a high level because of its potential for meeting crucial social needs. Resources should be as readily available for a Service which helps prevent young people from getting into trouble as for those services, such as Intermediate Treatment, which provide a rescue operation once that point has been reached. Secondly, funding of the statutory sector should be channelled through the usual policy-making network of the local authority department responsible for the Youth Service, and the growing in equality in funds reaching different areas should be reduced.

Implications for local authorities

10.26 The findings of our review of resources for the Youth Service have two main implications for local authorities. First, there needs to be good resource management, as outlined in chapter 8. All resources, whatever the origin of funding, must be subjected to proper methods of review and evaluation. Some authorities already ensure this, but it should be standard practice among all.

10.27 Secondly, authorities already do much to facilitate voluntaryism, but there are ways in which they might help to make it yet more effective. They can enhance the contribution that volunteers can make through good management and, for example, by giving financial assistance towards travelling expenses.

10.28 Authorities can assist voluntary bodies to be as effective as possible by maintaining officer support, so that they have capability for forward planning and responding to new needs, and by giving more help with premises. Whilst some already offer voluntary bodies the use of a wide range free of charge or at a heavily subsidised rate, others could do more to make educational premises easily and cheaply available for youth work. As pupil rolls fall, it may also be possible to offer youth organisations the use of school buildings which are wholly or partly redundant, although we recognise that there are pressures on authorities to dispose of these.

10.29 In the matter of capital grants to voluntary organisations, we would again urge all authorities to follow the good practice of some. We recognise that full responsibility for capital grants was devolved to authorities at a time when financial pressures made it difficult for them to increase their expenditure in this area. In view of the limited extent of the former DES system of grants, we would not feel justified in pressing for its reinstatement. We are nevertheless concerned that a reduction of capital grants below even their former level will lead to cumulative deterioration in the facilities that voluntary organisations can offer and may also deprive the Youth Service of voluntary funds that might otherwise be tapped. We hope therefore that authorities will in future be prepared to help fund both worthwhile new capital projects and schemes to improve or renovate existing premises. In order to do so, we suggest that they should explore the possibilities of joint funding with district councils, where they are not already doing so.

10.30　Apart from joint funding of capital projects, many district councils contribute to the Youth Service by offering financial assistance to voluntary bodies, and by making provision for sports and recreational facilities. (See 3.20.) These tend to be community facilities, shared by other age-groups besides young people. Whilst we welcome the practice of many district councils of offering young people concessions in charges for the use of such facilities, we would urge them also to ensure that youth organisations obtain a fair share of their use, particularly during the evenings.

Implications for voluntary bodies

10.31　We welcome the increasing efforts that voluntary bodies are making to raise funds, but we would urge them to give careful consideration to their priorities for using these. The temptation may be to devote as much as possible to work on the ground, but it should not be at the expense of ensuring an adequate managerial structure at the county or, where a number of counties can be adequately covered together, regional level. This has several important roles to perform, first, in monitoring and evaluating work in the field; secondly, in further developing effective liaison with local authorities in order to plan and co-ordinate the distribution of effort between the statutory and voluntary sectors (see 8.32 and 9.14); and, thirdly, in providing a recruitment and support network for volunteers. County or regional management of voluntary work is, however, unevenly resourced at present. Voluntary bodies will need to find the money to relate their management structures to those of authorities in order for liaison to be effective, and to ensure that officers are available for management tasks in all regions, sub-regions or counties. We recognise that finding money for such purposes is not easy, but voluntary bodies should preferably not rely solely on local authority funds for this.

Implications for the DES

10.32　For the reasons given in 10.25 above, we have found it impossible to determine whether funding for the Service should be more than at present. We welcome the inclusion of a line for the Youth Service in the annual White Paper on the Government's expenditure plans which seems to denote level funding up to 1983−84 at least. We believe that the policies which underlie planned expenditure on the Service should also be made clear, whatever changes may take place in block-grant machinery in the future.

10.33　We have already recommended (in 9.43−9.44) that those undertaking a course of initial training in youth work should receive mandatory grants.

114

Although the cost of these would fall on LEAs in the first instance, the DES would need to make provision for it in public expenditure plans.

10.34 Finally, there are two ways in which the DES could assist the voluntary sector more effectively through grant-aid, which can be earmarked for specific purposes. At present, grant-aid to national voluntary youth organisations is concentrated largely on headquarters administration and to a lesser extent on developmental and experimental projects. There is a continuing need for such aid, but we recommend that the DES should consider whether grant might be extended to regional and county levels of management (including bodies without a national parent organisation) and to experimental projects in managerial innovation, and accordingly enhanced. We believe this would be a cost-effective use of comparatively minor sums of money, which could be placed where needed at strategic points. It would enable the voluntary sector to improve its managerial capacity and thereby lead to the more effective deployment of resources in the field.

10.35 The second area in which we believe the DES should consider extending grant-aid is training. At present, grants are made for the initial training of youth and community workers at two institutions. We consider there would be value in aiding voluntary organisations themselves specifically to provide additional training programmes, particularly for part-time and volunteer staff.

10.36 *Summary of Recommendations*

   (1) Comprehensive statistics should be kept on a reliable, consistent and comparable basis for both the statutory and voluntary sectors. (10.1; see also 8.15)

   (2) The Youth Service should be funded at a high level. Resources should be available to develop work to counter urban deprivation, rural isolation and racism; full involvement in training schemes for the employed and unemployed; more opportunities for girls; and measures to integrate the handicapped. (10.24–10.25)

   (3) Machinery to monitor the effectiveness of the use of resources should be brought into being as part of the local and national structures discussed in chapter 8. (10.25). It should be standard practice among local authorities to ensure that all resources, whatever the origin of funding, are subjected to proper methods of review and evaluation. (10.26)

   (4) Funding of the statutory sector should be channelled through the usual policy-making network of the local authority department responsible for the Youth Service, and the growing inequality in funds reaching different areas should be reduced. (10.25)

   (5) Local authorities should continue to do all they can to support volunteers. (10.27)

   (6) Local authorities should assist voluntary bodies by maintaining officer support, by making more educational premises easily and cheaply available, and by funding new capital projects or schemes to improve or renovate existing premises. (10.28–10.29)

(7) District councils should ensure that youth organisations obtain a fair share of the use of community facilities. (10.30)

(8) Voluntary bodies should find funds to ensure that officers are available for management tasks in all regions, sub-regions or counties. (10.31)

(9) The DES should make clear the policies which underlie planned expenditure on the Youth Service. (10.32)

(10) The DES should make provision in public expenditure plans for mandatory grants for those undertaking initial training courses in youth work. (10.33)

(11) The DES should consider extending grant-aid to voluntary bodies to include:

    (*a*) management at regional and county levels, and projects in managerial innovation (10.34); and

    (*b*) training, particularly for part-time and volunteer staff. (10.35)

CHAPTER 11: THE NEED FOR LEGISLATION

Defects in the existing law; recent history of attempts to improve the situation; matters which a clause dealing with the Youth Service might cover; the possibility of future legislation dealing with further education powers and duties.

11.1 As we have observed in earlier chapters of this report, the lack of a clear statutory framework is a source of confusion and uncertainty of purpose, and is felt by many officers and workers in the field to imply an absence of public concern about the Youth Service. The words "Youth Service" do not in fact appear in any statute at all at the present time. The term was introduced by the Board of Education Circular 1486, issued at the beginning of World War II, which was directed towards meeting the needs of young people over the statutory school-leaving age (then 14) who were in a species of limbo pending their being called up into some branch of the war effort. After the War, Circular 13 (November 1944) deliberately extended the concept of the Youth Service to cover those still in full-time education, drawing authority for this purpose from Section 53 of the new Education Act 1944.

11.2 The two sections of the 1944 Act which are generally taken as conferring on local education authorities all necessary powers to provide such a Service, and indeed as imposing some kind of duty in respect of it, are sections 41 and 53, which, as amended, run as follows:

41. Subject as hereinafter provided, it shall be the duty of every local education authority to secure the provision for their area of adequate facilities for further education, that is to say:-

(a) full-time and part-time education for persons over compulsory school age; and

(b) leisure-time occupation, in such organised cultural training and recreative activities as are suited to their requirements, for any persons over compulsory school age who are able and willing to profit by the facilities provided for that purpose:

Provided that the provisions of this section shall not empower or require local education authorities to secure the provision of facilities for further education otherwise than in accordance with schemes of further education or at county colleges.

53. (1) It shall be the duty of every local education authority to secure that the facilities for primary secondary and further education provided for their area include adequate facilities for recreation and social and physical training, and for that purpose a local education authority, with the approval of the Secretary of State, may establish maintain and manage or assist the establishment, maintenance, and management of camps, holiday classes, playing fields, play centres, and other places (including playgrounds, gymnasiums, and swimming baths not appropriated to any school or college), at which facilities for recreation and for such training as aforesaid are available for persons receiving primary secondary or further education, and may organise games, expeditions and other activities for such persons, and may defray or contribute towards the expenses thereof.

(2) A local education authority, in making arrangements for the provision of facilities or the organisation of activities under the powers conferred on them by the last foregoing subsection shall, in particular, have regard to the expediency of co-operating with any voluntary societies or bodies whose objects include the provision of facilities or the organisation of activities of a similar character.

LEAs have done well in exploiting the existing statutory basis, but at the core of this there is an essential uncertainty which stands out in contrast with the rest of mainsteam education. Neither section provides a recognisable basis for the functions which the public has come to expect of the Youth Service. Section 53 is wider in the sense that it covers all stages of education, including further education, and mentions a whole aray of "facilities". Section 41 is perhaps more often quoted because it seems to refer more pointedly to the things that the Youth Service does, and includes the concept of "requirements"; but the proviso concerning "schemes for further education" (a concept without reality these past thirty years) weakens its force, and the "requirements" are nowhere defined. A better definition than either of these is needed for the objectives which LEAs and voluntary bodies are striving to meet in the Youth Service. At the same time, LEAs need to have their powers and duties more carefully defined; and the vital role of the voluntary sector needs more recognition than it gets in the rather anaemic subsection (2) of section 53.

11.3   It seems rational, in considering this problem, to start by reviewing other attempts to fill the hiatus left by existing legislation. The most recent was the Youth and Community Bill presented by Mr. Trevor Skeet MP in the 1979−80 session of Parliament, which was itself a reincarnation of earlier Bills put forward by Mr. Alan Haselhurst MP in 1973, Sir Edward Brown MP in 1974 and Mr. Cyril Townsend MP in 1975. It sought to require LEAs to prepare schemes for a range of services for young people and to specify the criteria to which they should have regard in making such schemes. In specifying the range of services, the Bill went as far as anyone has yet gone in trying to incorporate in an Act of Parliament the fundamental purpose of the Youth Service, viz:

"the provision and use of political and social education including the development of social and personal relationships and instruction as to the means of participating in the community" (clause 2(2) (a) as amended).

The Bill also sought to impose a number of very specific obligations on LEAs, apart from that of preparing schemes, namely:

(1) establishing standing joint committees with voluntary organisations and young people, for the purpose of preparing such schemes, encouraging the development of the services provided and co-ordinating them;

(2) assisting in the setting up of local youth councils for young people, wherever there was a local demand;

(3) encouraging young people to take part in community service, community development and community affairs;

(4) preparing schemes for the community use of schools and specifically for the maximum possible use by the community of all school facilities,

118

with a timetable for implementation (this clause was introduced at Committee stage); and

(5) extending the Youth Service "age-range".

It is probable that this very specificity was the Bill's downfall. It may well be that its prescriptive character robbed it of support which might have been forthcoming for a statute which allowed for more flexibility and local variation. The Government were in the end unable to accept it as formulated.

11.4 It seems that what is required is some legislative provision which will define the broad purposes of the Youth Service and give local authorties the necessary powers to employ staff, provide facilities and assist other bodies to this end. These powers should be no less wide than they are now. At the same time, local authorities should have a duty laid upon them, in respect of a defined age-range (involving for this purpose a definition of "young persons"), not necessarily to provide themselves a Service which will be sufficient in itself, but rather to see to it that an adequate Service is available in their areas, through one means or another. The precise means by which this is done should be left undefined, except that it should be done in effective and regular consultation with voluntary bodies and young people, thus recognising the essential roles which they play. In view of the variations in context, the difficulty of evaluating community needs and the importance of variety in local provision, it does not seem sensible to attempt to define the standard of such provision. We believe, however, that the statute might usefully mention a number of matters to which local authorities should have regard. These would not be prescriptive, but would be helpful in establishing the framework within which local authorities should work in carrying out their responsibilities.

11.5 For various reasons which we have traversed in 8.21, we believe that it would be appropriate to name local *education* authorities as the bodies to whom these powers and duties are given. We regard it as important that the Youth Service should be seen to be part of the mainstream of educational provision. Though we attach great importance to the dual nature of the Youth Service, we do not think that LEAs should be tied down as to the precise way in which they involve the voluntary sector and young people in a meaningful partnership. It should be sufficient, in our view, and the purposes and nature of local democracy would be best served, if they were obliged to consult regularly and effectively, having regard to certain considerations which would be specified but not made mandatory.

11.6 In the annex to this chapter we have set out a summary of the scope of a piece of legislation along these lines. We have neither the wish, nor the expertise, to draft the actual brief which would be needed by the Parliamentary draftsmen. This is a task for the Department of Education and Science. Our formulation is intended simply to state clearly what such legislation would actually do. We wish here, however, to note two points. First, it will be observed that our formulation makes no mention of schemes. The concept of a scheme, to be made by a LEA and approved by the Secretary of State, seems to us a rather interesting way of avoiding the need for a definition of function. It is a legislative concept which seems to us was more popular in the days of the 1944 Act than it is likely to be today: it seems more in tune with present-day thinking to try to frame a defi-nition-of the task to be performed. Secondly, it seems to us that all the essential objectives, as set out in the annex, could be comprised within a single (admittedly long and fairly complex) clause. This may be a helpful consideration when it comes to seeking an appropriate vehicle for such a legislative provision. We understand that consideration is being given to the need for a Bill which would clarify the position of LEAs in respect of the provision of further education. (This may be necessary because of the obsolescence of the scheme procedure mentioned above). If such a measure is being prepared, it seems inconceivable that it should not deal also with powers and duties in respect of the Youth Service (if only because, at the moment, the latter is subsumed under the former). We hope that the proposals we make in this chapter may be accepted as the basis of an appropriate clause in such a Bill.

11.7 *Summary of recommendations*

Legislation as set out in the following annex should be introduced to define the broad purposes of the Youth Service and give local authorities the necessary powers to employ staff, provide facilities and assist other bodies to this end.

ANNEX TO CHAPTER 11

Objects to be achieved by legislation dealing with the powers and duties of LEAs in relation to the Youth Service.

1. Local education authorities should continue to have a power, no less wide than they have at present under sections 41 and 53 of the Education Act 1944, to provide facilities for social, physical, cultural and recreational activities suited to the requirements of all persons who wish to use them, irrespective of their age.

2. It should be the duty of every local education authority, as part of its educa-tional functions
   (a) to assess the need for and secure the provision of facilities, outside full-time education and employment, whereby young people may be assisted to discover their own resources of mind and body, to understand the society of which they form part, to have access to information and skills requisite for playing a full part in that society, and to make a contri-bution to the economic and social life of their community;
   (b) in assessing such need and in securing such provision, to ensure that there is effective and regular consultation with voluntary organisations which provide services for young people in the area, and with young people themselves; and
   (c) to ensure in association with other local education authorities and with voluntary organisations that persons are available for working with young people whether in a full-time, part-time, or voluntary capacity; and that opportunities are available for such persons to receive initial and in-service training.

For the purpose of these requirements, "young people" should be defined as those who have attained the age of 11 years and have not yet attained the age of 21.

3.   In carrying out these duties every local education authority should take account of all the young people in their area, and not just those who are members of a youth club or organisation, and should have regard to the following:

(a) securing the provision of appropriate information, advice and counselling;

(b) enabling and encouraging young people to set up and run their own activities and organisations;

(c) enabling and encouraging young people to be involved in the community;

(d) assisting young people to make the transition from school to work, and meeting the needs of young people who are unemployed;

(e) meeting the needs of girls and young women;

(f) meeting the needs of young people who belong to ethnic communities;

(g) meeting the needs of young people who suffer from mental or physical handicap; and

(h) promoting international visits and understanding.

CHAPTER 12:   SUMMARY OF RECOMMENDATIONS

We here recapitulate the recommendations which we have made in each chapter, grouping them under headings which indicate their nature and purpose.

CHAPTER 5:   CRITICAL APPRAISAL OF THE YOUTH SERVICE

Tasks and Methods

1   The Youth Service has the duty to help all young people who have need of it. (5.2)

2   The Youth Service's task is to provide social education. It has developed specific methods of working, including the experiential curriculum, voluntaryism, a non-authoritative relationship between workers and young people, and encouraging young people to participate in decision-making. All these modes of operation should be brought into play. (5.5–5.6)

3   LEAs and voluntary bodies, in partnership, should ensure a more equitable geographical spread of Youth Service provision. (5.12)

4   Provision for the over-16s is an urgent requirement. (5.13)

5   Participation by young people should be strengthened at all levels—in activity groups, clubs, local affairs, national youth organisations and at the national and international levels. It may follow a variety of patterns. (5.19–5.22)

6   An assured place should be given to provision of information, advice and counselling within planning of local provision. The providing authorities should give thought to this, and ensure that funding is on a regular and systematic basis. (5.28–5.29)

7   Community involvement should be available for all young people with maximum freedom of choice and opportunity. (5.33)

8   The provision of political education should be a normal part of the Youth Service curriculum, pursued in such ways as to involve active participation. Ways to bring this about include more attention to political education in training courses and active consideration at a national and local level, especially involving management committees. (5.36–5.41)

9   Youth workers should build awareness of the international context into their work. (5.46)

CHAPTER 6:   CHALLENGE AND RESPONSE

Needs and Other Agencies

1   The Youth Service and other services dealing with young people should develop the means of working together. It is the responsibility of management to foster collaborative arrangements with other services, whilst respecting the independence and proper role of each. This will encourage the most effective use of funds, staff and facilities. (6.3–6.10)

2   The Youth Service has an essential role in helping to provide facilities and activities for unemployed young people; in sustaining their social confidence, skills and motivation; and in making a contribution, including the sponsorship of courses, to the planning, delivery and management of the Youth Training Scheme. Provision will be needed for those young people for whom no suitable training is available, who are still unemployed after training, or who find themselves in dead-end employment. (6.11−6.18)

3   Converging aims and methods make it all the more necessary that the Youth Service should contribute to the work and curriculum of schools and colleges. (6.19−6.26)

4   There is a special need for co-ordinated management in the inner cities. (6.27−6.29)

5   In rural areas, attention should be paid to providing equitable funding and appropriate styles of provision. (6.30−6.34)

6   The Youth Service in common with other agencies and services has a duty to combat racism in all its forms. (6.35−6.42)

7   The needs of ethnic communities should be recognised in the planning, management and delivery of local youth provision. (6.43−6.49)

8   The Service should take deliberate steps to ensure that the personal development of girls is not hindered by confused or reactionary attitudes to the role of women in society or by sexist attitudes in the Service itself. The personal development needs of girls in mixed settings may need to be catered for by an increase, for a time, in separate provision. (6.50−6.54)

9   The integration of handicapped young people into the community implies a variety of provision, both integrated and separate. (6.55−6.60)

CHAPTER 7:   A YOUTH SERVICE FOR THE 1980s

Objectives, Offerings and Age-Ranges

1   The overall aims of the Youth Service should be seen as affirming an individual's self-belief and encouraging participation in society. (7.3−7.5)

2   The Youth Service needs to acknowledge the need for the spiritual development of the individual. (7.6)

3   The mainstream offerings of the Youth Service by which it will achieve these aims are *association* (a place to meet); *activities*; *advice*, information and counselling; means to *action* in the community; and *access* to vocational and life skills. (7.7−7.13)

4   Local education authorities should continue to have the power to provide, or

123

to assist other services to provide, for the whole age-group of young people. Statutory duties should embrace the ages 11–20. (7.14–7.18)

CHAPTER 8:   STRUCTURES

Management at National and Local Level

1   The four basic management functions of setting objectives, assigning roles, allocating resources, and monitoring performance require appropriate structures for their fulfilment at national and local level. (8.2)

2   The function of setting objectives for the Youth Service at national level could appropriately by fulfilled by means of legislation. (8.3)

3   A Minister should be designated, based in the DES, to co-ordinate the work of all departments which have an interest in youth affairs. (8.4)

4   An advisory council should be appointed to advise Ministers on youth affairs. It should consist of a small number of individuals appointed in a personal and non-representative capacity, broadly reflecting a wide range of youth interests. It should be serviced by the DES but have a distinct public identity. (8.10)

5   The terms of reference and organisational structure of the National Youth Bureau should be reviewed to enable it to carry out more effectively the tasks of collecting and analysing data about youth affairs and of spreading information about good practice and innovation. (8.17–8.19)

6   At local level the local education authority should be recognised as the prime focus for youth affairs and should be given a statutory responsibility for co-ordination in respect of the services of the local authority itself, as between different tiers of local government, and as between local authority services and the voluntary sector. (8.21–8.22)

7   LEAs should be given a statutory duty to create machinery to ensure regular and effective communication and consultation with voluntary youth organisations, over the whole field of the four management functions. The precise form of this machinery should not be prescribed: scope should be left for local variation. (8.29–8.31)

8   Voluntary youth organisations in an area should take steps to ensure that they have the capability of acting collectively in identifying and working out policy issues and playing their part in a partnership with the LEA. Local consortia, such as the present Councils for Voluntary Youth Services, may be appropriate for this purpose. (8.31)

9   In order to function effectively, such a consortium will need administrative and staff support, which may well involve a specific appointment. It should not be assumed that this function will be undertaken by an officer of the LEA. (8.32)

10   We attach importance to the role of local youth councils and to the effective involvement of young people in local decision-making structures. (8.34)

11   At the centre of the local structure there should be a joint committee to which specific functions and powers should be delegated by the local authority. On it, representatives of voluntary organisations, of young people and of the local authority should work together to frame and review policy and to monitor performance. (8.35)

12   Youth Service organisations and personnel should be actively involved in local arrangements for the planning and delivery of the proposed Youth Training Scheme, both as members of local boards and as managing agencies and sponsors. (8.38−8.39)

CHAPTER 9:   STAFFING AND TRAINING

Staffing

1   Workers should accept as essential parts of their work both managerial work, involving personnel work and administration, and face-to-face work, involving work with young people and community development. These four functions should be reflected in their training. (9.1)

2   More needs to be done to correct the balance of representation of women and ethnic minorities, especially amongst full-time workers and at officer level. (9.4−9.5)

3   Management should give thought to finding means of easing the problem of maintaining morale among full-time workers in a small and open-ended service, e.g. by facilitating transfers and by extending the career structure. (9.9−9.10)

4   Part-timers provide special skills and links with the local community, and have special briefing and supervision needs. (9.16−9.17)

5   Volunteers are a special feature of the Youth Service but their contribution cannot be taken for granted. Special efforts have to be made to recruit and retain them. (9.18−9.21)

Training

6   There is a clear and urgent need for a national supervisory panel to accredit and monitor both initial and in-service training for full-time staff. It should be concerned with supply as well as training. (9.30)

7   Consideration should be given to the acceptance of qualified teachers as qualified youth workers only after an assessment of the training they have undertaken or are prepared to take. The youth option in B Ed courses should be developed and expanded. (9.34−9.35)

8   Urgent consideration should be given to the development of many areas of probation, professional support and in-service training. (9.37−9.40)

125

9   Mandatory grants should be available for those undertaking a course of initial training for the Youth Service. (9.43–9.44)

10   Training programmes for part-time staff and volunteers should continue to be developed on a local basis, but a moderating and co-ordinating role should be undertaken by Regional Advisory Councils. (9.50)

CHAPTER 10:   RESOURCES

1   Comprehensive statistics should be kept on a reliable, consistent and comparable basis for both the statutory and voluntary sectors. (10.1; see also 8.15)

2   The Youth Service should be funded at a high level. Resources should be available to develop work to counter urban deprivation, rural isolation and racism; full involvement in training schemes for the employed and unemployed; more opportunities for girls; and measures to integrate the handicapped. (10.24–10.25)

3   Machinery to monitor the effectiveness of the use of resources should be brought into being as part of the local and national structures discussed in chapter 8. (10.25). It should be standard practice among local authorities to ensure that all resources, whatever the origin of funding, are subjected to proper methods of review and evaluation. (10.26)

4   Funding of the statutory sector should be channelled through the usual policy-making network of the local authority department responsible for the Youth Service, and the growing inequality in funds reaching different areas should be reduced. (10.25)

5   Local authorities should continue to do all they can to support volunteers. (10.27)

6   Local authorities should assist voluntary bodies by maintaining officer support, by making more educational premises easily and cheaply available, and by funding new capital projects or schemes to improve or renovate existing premises. (10.28–10.29)

7   District councils should ensure that youth organisations obtain a fair share of the use of community facilities. (10.30)

8   Voluntary bodies should find funds to ensure that officers are available for management tasks in all regions, sub-regions or counties. (10.31)

9   The DES should make clear the policies which underlie planned expenditure on the Youth Service. (10.32)

10   The DES should make provision in public expenditure plans for mandatory grants for those undertaking initial training courses in youth work. (10.33)

11   The DES should consider extending grant-aid to voluntary bodies to include:

(a) management at regional and county levels, and projects in managerial innovation (10.34); and

(b) training, particularly for part-time and volunteer staff. (10.35)

CHAPTER 11:   LEGISLATION

Legislation as set out in the annex to chapter 11 should be introduced to define the broad purposes of the Youth Service and give local authorities the necessary powers to employ staff, provide facilities and assist other bodies to this end.

APPENDIX A: MEMBERSHIP OF THE REVIEW GROUP

Outside appointments shown are those held by members on being appointed to the Review Group.

Chairman:	Mr. A. Thompson CB	Formerly Deputy Secretary, Department of Education and Science.
Members:	Revd. E. F. Cattermole	Director of the National Council for Voluntary Youth Services
	Mr. J. Collins	Chairperson, British Youth Council.
	Mr. A. B. Hampton TD DL	Chairman, Record Ridgeway Ltd, Sheffield; President of the Engineering Employers' Federation
	Mr. E. Hopwood	Senior Education Officer, EssexCountyCouncil.
	Mr. W. R. Knight	Director of Educational Services, City of Bradford MetropolitanCouncil.
	Ms. J. D. J. McKenley	Lecturer in careers education, Hackney College, London (appointedFebruary1982).
	Mrs. J. Walpole	Chairman, Norfolk County Council Education Committee.

APPENDIX B: LIST OF BODIES AND INDIVIDUALS WHO GAVE EVIDENCE

Submissions made by local groups or individuals through a parent or employing organisation have not necessarily been included separately.

1. Local Education Authorities and Associations

Association of County Councils
Association of Metropolitan Authorities
Avon County Council

Barking and Dagenham London Borough Council
Barnet London Borough Council
Barnsley Metropolitan Borough Council
Bedfordshire County Council
Berkshire County Council
Bexley London Borough Council
Birmingham Metropolitan City Council
Bolton Metropolitan Borough Council
Bradford Metropolitan City Council
Bromley London Borough Council
Buckinghamshire County Council

Calderdale Metropolitan Borough Council
Cambridgeshire County Council
Cheshire County Council
Cleveland County Council
Cornwall County Council
Coventry Metropolitan City Council
Croydon London Borough Council
Cumbria County Council

Derbyshire County Council
Devon County Council
Doncaster Metropolitan Borough Council
Dorset County Council
Dudley Metropolitan Borough Council
Durham County Council

Ealing London Borough Council
Enfield London Borough Council
Essex County Council
Essex County Council : additional evidence from Thurrock Area

Gateshead Metropolitan Borough Council
Gloucestershire County Council

Harringey London Borough Council
Harrow London Borough Council
Havering London Borough Council
Hereford and Worcester County Council
Hertfordshire County Council
Hillingdon London Borough Council

Hounslow London Borough Council
Humberside County Council

Inner London Education Authority
Isle of Wight County Council

Kent County Council
Kingston-upon-Thames Royal Borough Council
Kirklees Metropolitan Council
Knowsley Metropolitan Borough Council

Lancashire County Council
Leicester County Council
Lincolnshire County Council
Liverpool City Council

Manchester City Council
Merton London Borough Council

Newcastle-upon-Tyne City Council
Newham London Borough Council
Norfolk County Council
North Tyneside Metropolitan Borough Council
North Yorkshire County Council
Northamptonshire County Council
Northumberland County Council
Nottinghamshire County Council

Oldham Metropolitan Borough Council
Oxfordshire County Council

Redbridge London Borough Council
Rochdale Metropolitan Borough Council
Rotherham Metropolitan Borough Council

Salford City Council
Sandwell Metropolitan Borough Council
Sefton Metropolitan Borough Council
Sheffield City Council
Shropshire County Council
Solihull Metropolitan Borough Council
Somerset County Council
South Tyneside Metropolitan Borough Council
Staffordshire County Council
Stockport Metropolitan Borough Council
Suffolk County Council
Sunderland Metropolitan Borough Council
Surrey County Council
Sutton London Borough Council

Wakefield Metropolitan District Council
Walsall Metropolitan Borough Council
Waltham Forest London Borough Council
Warwickshire County Council
West Sussex County Council

Wigan Metropolitan Borough Council
Wiltshire County Council
Wirral Metropolitan Borough Council
Wolverhampton Metropolitan Borough Council

2. Local Authorities (Non-LEA)

Arun District Council
Ashford Borough Council

Babergh District Council
Blythe Valley Borough Council
Bournemouth Borough Council
Brentwood District Council

Cambridge City Council
Camden London Borough Council
Carrick District Council
Castle Morpeth Borough Council
Chester City Council
Christchurch Borough Council
Cleethorpes Borough Council
Copeland Borough Council
Corby District Council
Cotswold District Council

Darlington Borough Council
Dartford Borough Council
Derby City Council

East Lindsey District Council
East Yorkshire Borough Council
Epping Forest District Council

Forest of Dean District Council

Gedling Borough Council
Gillingham Borough Council
Gloucester City Council
Guildford Borough Council

Hammersmith and Fulham London Borough Council
Harborough District Council
Harlow Council
Hart District Council
Hartlepool City Council
Hereford City Council
Hinckley and Bosworth District Council
Hove Borough Council

Kensington and Chelsea Royal Borough Council
Kerrier District Council

Leicester City Council
Lewisham London Borough Council

Maidstone Borough Council
Milton Keynes Borough Council
Mole Valley District Council

New Forest District Council
North Bedfordshire Borough Council
North Cornwall District Council
North Dorset District Council
Norwich City Council
Nottingham City Council
Nuneaton and Bedworth Borough Council

Pendle Borough Council
Plymouth City Council
Poole Borough Council

Reigate and Banstead Borough Council
Rugby Borough Council
Runnymede Borough Council

St. Edmundsbury Borough Council
Scunthorpe Borough Council
Slough Corporation
South Bucks District Council
South Norfolk District Council
Southampton City Council
Southend-on-Sea Borough Council
Southwark London Borough Council
Stoke-on-Trent City Council

Thamesdown Borough Council
Thanet District Council

Warrington Borough Council
Waverley District Council
West Norfolk District Council
West Somerset District Council
Westminster City Council
Winchester City Council
Wokingham District Council

3. National Voluntary Organisations

Army Cadet Force Association

Boys' Brigade
British Association of Settlements and Social Action Centres
British Pregnancy Advisory Service
British Red Cross Society
British Youth Council

Centreprise Trust
Community Projects Foundation
Community Service Volunteers
Council for Environmental Conservation Youth Unit

Disabled Living Foundation
Duke of Edinburgh's Award

Endeavour Training

Frontier Youth Trust

Girl Guides Association
Girls' Brigade
Girls' Venture Corps

National Association for the Care and Resettlement of Offenders
National Associatoin of Boys' Clubs
National Association of Youth Clubs
National Children's Centre
National Council for Voluntary Organisations
National Council for Voluntary Youth Services
National Federation of Young Farmers' Clubs
National Youth Bureau

Ocean Youth Club

Physically Handicapped and Able Bodied
Pony Club

St. John Ambulance Association and Brigade
Save the Children Fund
Scout Association
Sea Cadet Association

Young Men's Christian Associations—National Council
Young Ornithologists' Club
Young Women's Christian Association of Great Britain
Youth Call
Youth Choice
Youth Development Trust
Youth Hostels Association
Youth Service Partners

4. Regional and Local Voluntary Organisations

Avon Council for Voluntary Youth Services

Barnet Borough Conference of Voluntary Youth Organisations
Barnsley District Council for Voluntary Service
Berkshire Association of Boys' Clubs
Berkshire Association of Youth Clubs
Berkshire Council of Voluntary Youth Service
Berkshire County Scout Council
Berkshire Girl Guides Association
Berkshire St. John Ambulance Brigade
Birmingham Young Volunteers
Bradford Council for Voluntary Service
Brighton Young Volunteers
Buckinghamshire Council for Voluntary Youth Services

133

Chesterfield Task Force
Cleveland Youth Association
Community Industry, Hull
Cumbria Council for Voluntary Youth Services

Devon Council for Voluntary Youth Services
Dover Volunteer Group
Durham County Badminton Assóciation Youth Squad

East Midlands Play Association
East Sussex Council for Voluntary Youth Services
Enfield Scout Assocation
Enfield Voluntary Youth Organisations
Essex Council for Voluntary Youth Services

Folkus, Durham

Gateshead District Scout Association
Girl Guides Association, North-East Region
Gloucestershire Council for Voluntary Youth Servivces
Greater London—South-East County Scout Council
Greater London Standing Conference of Voluntary Youth Organisations
Greater Manchester Youth Association

Hereford and Worcester Army Cadet Force
Hereford and Worcester Council for Voluntary Youth Service
Herefordshire Federation of Young Farmers' Clubs
Herefordshire Girl Guides Association
Hertfordshire Association of Youth Clubs
Hertfordshire Standing Conference on Drug Mis-use
Humberside Council for Voluntary Youth Services
Humberside Youth Association

Isle of Wight Scout Association

Kent Council for Voluntary Youth Services

Lancashire Council for Voluntary Youth Services
Leeds Council for Voluntary Service
Leicestershire Council for Voluntary Youth Services
Lincolnshire Council for Voluntary Youth Services

Merseyside Youth Association

Norfolk Council for Voluntary Youth Services
Northamptonshire Boys' Clubs
Northamptonshire Council for Voluntary Youth Service
North Devon Community Action
Northern Area Ramblers' Association
Northumberland Standing Conference of Voluntary Youth Organisations
Nottingham Young Volunteers

Sevenoaks Voluntary Service Unit
Sheffield Council of Voluntary Youth Service
Shropshire Council for Voluntary Youth Services

Slough District Scout Council
Solihull Young National Trust
Somerset and South Avon Federation of Young Farmers' Clubs
Somerset Council for Voluntary Youth Services
Stafford District Voluntary Services
Suffolk Association of Youth
Suffolk Council for Voluntary Youth Services
Surrey Association of Youth Clubs and Surrey Physically Handicapped and
    Able Bodied
Sussex Youth Association

Thamesdown Voluntary Service Council, Wiltshire

Welwyn Hatfield Young Volunteers
West End Co-ordinated Voluntary Services for Homeless Single People,
    London
Worcestershire Federation of Young Farmers' Clubs
Worcestershire Girl Guides Association

Youth Action, Tameside
Youth in Action, Sutton

5. Other Local Youth Organisations, Clubs and Units

Avon

Three Lamps Methodist Youth Club, Bristol

Berkshire

Caversham Park Village Association
Wokingham Methodist Youth Club

Cambridgeshire

St Neots Centre, Huntingdon
Save the Children, Cambridge Project

Cheshire

Halton Lodge Youth Club, Runcorn

Devon

Whipton Youth Club, Exeter

Dorset

Harewood Centre, Bournemouth

East Sussex

Elm Court Centre, Seaford

Essex

Druid Venture Scout Group, Southend

Gloucestershire
Bisley Youth Club
Dursley Shell Group
Fairford Youth Club
Lonsdale Methodist Youth Club, Gloucester
Northway Club, Tewkesbury
Roxburgh House Youth Club
Sitmoc—Young People's Fellowship, Cheltenham
Soudley Youth Club
Stonehouse Community Centre
Winchcombe Youth Club
Wotton-under-Edge Youth Club

Greater Manchester
Firswood & District Community Association

Hampshire
2nd Aldershot Venture Scout Unit
Chandlers Ford Methodist Youth Club, Eastleigh
Romsey Methodist Youth Club
Weston Park Centre, Southampton

Hertfordshire
Sea Rangers Assocation, Potters Bar

Humberside
Snaith Boys' Club, Goole
Snaith Girls' Friendly Society, Goole

Kent
Culverstone Community Association, Meopham
Faversham County Youth Club
Maidstone YMCA
St Thomas' Youth Club, Canterbury
Showfields Youth Club, Tunbridge Wells

Lincolnshire
Grantham Play Association

London Borough of Enfield
Enfield Churches' (Noah's Ark) Open Youth Centre
33rd Enfield Guides
10th Enfield Sea Scouts
Enfield Youth Theatre
4th New Southgate Guide Company and Brownie Pack

London Borough of Greenwich
Greenwich Voluntary Workers' Bureau

London Borough of Islington
Springboard, Islington

London Borough of Merton
7th Morden Scouts
8th Morden Scouts

London Borough of Newham
Carpenters' and Dockland Centre
Church Army Hartley Centre
Eastlea Centre, Canning Town
Fairbairn House Boys Club, Plaistow
Kensington Youth Centre
Little Eye Club, Manor Park
Shipman Youth Centre

London Borough of Southwark
Southwark Community Development Project for the Mentally Handicapped

London Borough of Wandsworth
Balham Job & Training Workshop
Springfield Methodist Youth Club

Merseyside
Great Georges Project, Liverpool
Worcester Youth Centre, Bootle

North Yorkshire
Pocklington Youth Centre, York

Northamptonshire
Abington Community Association, Northampton

Northumberland
Buffalo Youth Club, Blyth
Cramlington Detached Youth Project
Cramlington Village Community Centre
Seaton Delaval Youth Club, Whitley Bay
South Beach Youth Club

Somerset
Lighthouse Methodist Youth Club, Burnham-on-Sea

South Yorkshire
Barnsley Sea Cadet Corps
Beckett Centre, Barnsley
Bolton-on-Dearne Church Lads' & Church Girls' Brigade
Elsecar Parish Church Open Youth Club
Willowgarth Youth Club
Young People's Interest Group, Barnsley

Surrey

Fairlands Youth Club, Guildford
Haslemere Methodist Youth Club

Tyne & Wear

Beth Jacobs Girls' Club, Gateshead
Blaydon & District Swimming & Life-Saving Club
1509 (Blaydon) Squadron, Air Training Corps
Caprian Amateur Dramatic & Operatic Society, Gateshead
Christchurch Youth Club, Felling
Fellside Junior Tennis Club
Gateshead Amateur Swimming Club
Gateshead Battalion Boys' Brigade
Gateshead East Primary Athletics Assocation
Gateshead Sea Cadet Corps
Gateshead 2nd Scout Group
Gateshead 8th Scout Group
Gateshead 9th Scout Group
Gateshead 12th Scout Group
Gateshead 15th Scout Group
Gateshead 19th Scout Group
Gateshead 22nd Scout Group
Gateshead 26th Scout Group
Gateshead 33rd Scout Group
Gateshead Trampoline Club
Hertfordshire House Community Assocation, Gateshead
Quykham Venture Scout Unit, Newcastle
Redheugh Boys Club
St Theresa's Club for Handicapped Children, Gateshead
Smailes Lane Youth Club, Rowlands Gill
South Shields YMCA
Whickham Badminton Club
Whickham Choral Union
Whickham Tennis Club
1st Windy Nook Girls' Brigade Company
Windy Nook Methodist Junior and Youth Clubs
Winlaton Centre Badminton Club
Winlaton Centre Netball Club

West Midlands

All Saints Youth Club, Sedgley
Quarry Bank Community Association, Brierley Hill
Tipton Green Methodist Boys' Club

West Yorkshire

Canterbury Avenue Youth & Community Assocation
Earlsheaton High School, Kirklees
Netherton Youth Centre, Huddersfield
Phoenix Youth Centre, Huddersfield
R. M. Grylls Youth Club, Liversedge